UNDERSTANDING

THE
PONY

YOUR **GUIDE** TO HORSE HEALTH
CARE AND MANAGEMENT

UNDERSTANDING

THE
PONY

YOUR **GUIDE** TO HORSE HEALTH
CARE AND MANAGEMENT

Karen Briggs

ECLIPSE
PRESS

Essex, Connecticut

An imprint of Globe Pequot, the trade division of
The Rowman & Littlefield Publishing Group, Inc.
4501 Forbes Blvd., Ste. 200
Lanham, MD 20706
www.rowman.com

Distributed by NATIONAL BOOK NETWORK

British Library Cataloguing in Publication Information available

Library of Congress Cataloging-in-Publication Data Available
ISBN 978-1-4930-7471-6 (paper : alk. paper)

∞™ The paper used in this publication meets the minimum
requirements of American National Standard for Information
Sciences—Permanence of Paper for Printed Library Materials,
ANSI/NISO Z39.48-1992.

Contents

INTRODUCTION

I first fell in love with a pony when I was 10 years old. I was spending two weeks at a summer riding camp — my first time away from my parents for any length of time — and I was assigned a patient partner in a little bay mare called Holly. She was about 13 hands, more horizontally gifted than vertically, and in my mind's eye I can recall she had a star in the shape of a lady's fan on her forehead and the most amazing liquid eyes. At Camp Saddlewood, she was to be "mine" to ride twice a day, for 14 whole days — what bliss! I was instantly head over heels. Holly took astonishingly good care of me through my first camp experience and again the following summer, though by that time I was beginning to outgrow her. Her impeccable "school horse" instincts kept my graceless beginner body on board even when it had no real right to be there, tolerated my unintentional insults to her mouth and her back…and though she wasn't above teaching me a lesson in humility when required, clearly she had baby sat many awkward kids like me in the past. For my part, I was enchanted just to spend time around a pony who was Almost Mine; I would spend countless hours grooming her and watching her munch hay, swish flies, or just doze in the afternoon hours between lessons.

When my parents pulled in to Saddlewood to witness our

end-of-session horse show and take me home, I couldn't wait to show Holly to them. Evidently they didn't share my opinion of her great beauty; my mother noted her rather generous ears and dubbed her "the mule!" Though I was gravely wounded by this remark, it didn't alter my passion; the little bay mare had gotten me hooked for life. There were to be many more ponies in my young life, teachers all; and when I was 16, I was finally able to achieve my most heartfelt ambition: a horse of my own. His name was Pokey, and he was a pony, too; descended from Arabian and Quarter Horse parents, he stood 14.2 hands and was perfectly suited, size-wise, to my modest 5'2" height. Our beginnings together were far from smooth, however. I wasn't nearly as accomplished a rider as I'd thought, and Pokey was only half-trained and possessed of a number of naughty habits, including barn-sourness, spookiness, and a tremendous buck!

But we ironed out the rough patches and soon developed a deep and abiding affection, while dabbling in virtually every kind of equestrian activity, from endurance riding to Western pleasure to dressage and eventing. At our local boarding stable, Pokey became known as the "do-everything" pony.

I'm happy to say that Pokey is still with me, at the age of 29. His worth to me is beyond description. Having gone on to ride many larger and more athletically inclined Thoroughbreds and warmbloods, my appreciation for Pokey and all he taught me continues to deepen. When all is said and done, I owe my riding career to ponies, and so ponies remain a passion. That's why this book has been written. Because this story is an ordinary one; it happens all over the world on a regular basis. I hope all of you who appreciate ponies will find something here to inform you, amuse you, or help you in your relationship with the smaller equines — who may have the biggest hearts of all.

Karen Briggs
Orangeville, Ontario, Canada

CHAPTER 1
What is a Pony?

What is a pony, as opposed to a horse? Zoologists don't recognize a difference — from a taxonomic point of view, both horses and ponies are *Equus callabus*, descended from the same evolutionary tree. But horsemen the world over classify ponies separately from horses. What's the distinction?

Horses are something of an artificial construct, if the truth be told — the result of hundreds of years of humans selectively breeding for greater height, speed, or strength. Often they have suffered something of a trade off in the process, losing their natural hardiness, disease resistance, and some of the wild instincts that helped protect the original wild equines from predators and harsh weather.

Most pony breeds, in contrast, evolved in the most inhospitable of conditions — on windswept islands, on high snowy steppes, in bogs and marshes — and today they retain the qualities that have helped ensure their survival through the millennia. Thick, shaggy manes and tails, and heavy winter coats, still protect them from the elements; iron-hard little hooves remain nimble over rocks and uneven terrain; a compact size helps conserve body heat; and an energy-saving metabolism allows them to stay plump and sassy on even the poorest of forages. In fact, ponies could be considered the natural descendants of ancient wild "horses," which, fossil records show, were actually pony-sized. And they remain the closest relations of the remaining wild equines: the Tarpan and Przewalski's horse. One only has to look at a Shetland pony in his natural state to begin to understand how close ponies are to these "primitive" animals. Domestication is a fine line at the best of times, and if ponies are perhaps more "primitive" than their larger cousins, horses, they are also, without a doubt, survivors.

> ## AT A GLANCE
>
> • Ponies are defined by their size. A height of 14.2 hands (58 inches, or 146 centimeters) at the withers is generally considered to be the cut-off point between horse and pony.
>
> • Unlike many horse breeds, most pony breeds have an inherent hardiness because of conditions in which they evolved.
>
> • Ponies are recognized for their intelligence.

Physically, ponies share a few characteristics that distinguish them from horses. Their legs tend to be proportionately shorter, their barrels and backs wider, their withers less prominent, and their heads shorter and broader, with wide-set eyes. Conformation does vary somewhat from breed to breed, of course, but other qualities, such as sure-footedness, the ability to survive on the poorest feed, and longevity (many ponies live well into their 30s or even 40s), seem to be universal.

Less easy to quantify, but recognized nonetheless, is the unique intelligence of the pony. There are no studies to define it, yet if you ask any horseperson who's ever had a close encounter with a pony, he or

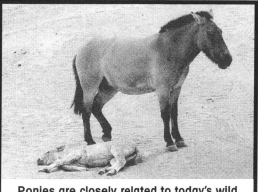

Ponies are closely related to today's wild equines, including Przewalski's horse.

she will readily acknowledge that ponies have a wily intelligence quite different from that of most horses. Being more clever than their predators is one of the qualities that has kept ponies alive on the moors, plains, and deserts over the centuries — but today, the phrase "too smart for his own good" is regularly applied to ponies that seem more interested in being cheeky and devious than in cooperating with humans! Woe betide any trainer who approaches a pony thinking he's a "lesser being" than a horse; he'll likely be taught a valuable lesson in respect. The innate intelligence of ponies has earned them a reputation for being "difficult," but it's really not deserved; most ponies have naturally gentle dispositions, but might be described (at the risk of anthropomorphizing) as having a merry sense of humor.

Size, intelligence, and hardiness define ponies.

They can hardly be blamed for occasionally taking advantage of humanity's weaker moments!

All of these characteristics rolled together define ponies across the planet and distinguish them from horses. But we also can define ponies merely by their size, without regard to their ancestry or conformation. A height of 14 hands, two inches (58 inches, or 146 centimeters) at the withers is considered, in most countries, to be the cut-off point between horse and pony. Any animal standing up to, and including 14.2 hands, is described as a pony; anything over 14.2 is a horse. This is a useful definition for the purposes of the show ring, where ponies and horses usually compete separately. It also can be a source of some confusion. Many animals that are genetically "horse" but are of small stature end up being classified as ponies, while individuals of pony breeding that grow larger than usual may end up being called horses. There are a number of breeds that straddle the height limit; Arabians, Morgans, and Quarter Horses, to name only three, often produce pony-sized individuals even though there is little or no "pony blood" in any of these breeds. Connemara and Highland ponies, when provided with good nutrition, may end up as tall as 15 to 15.2 hands — by show standards, horses, but by breed standards, still ponies.

Adding to the confusion is the fact that some breeds are always described as horses, even though they come under the pony height limit. Icelandics, for example, though stunted by centuries of harsh living in the North Atlantic, are descended from Viking horses and thus are always referred to as horses despite their average size of 13.3 hands. Miniatures, too, though they are the tiniest of all equines, are described as horses because of the horse-like proportions of the best individuals. At the other end of the spectrum are polo "ponies" — almost invariably horse-sized, but called ponies nonetheless. Clearly, the terminology used for horses and ponies is as clear as mud!

Regardless of how you define a pony, however, there's no denying the popularity of smaller equines. Practically every country has a native pony breed (or two, or — in the case of the United Kingdom — eleven or twelve!), and the vast majority of today's internationally competitive riders first learned to ride on a pony. Sports where ponies can show off their athletic prowess are booming as well, as we'll see in future chapters.

Despite all the evolutionary advantages that equip ponies to survive admirably well on their own, they have chosen to ally themselves with mankind — so it's well worth returning the favor by providing them with good care and much appreciation for their talents. Consider this book a celebration of ponies, and their cherished place in our lives.

CHAPTER 2

Breeds of Ponies

Circumstance, climate, and selective breeding have developed hundreds of different breeds of ponies around the world. Many have origins lost in the mists of time, though a few have only emerged in the past century and are no less popular for having had a short history. It would be next to impossible to acquaint you with every single breed of pony, but here are some of the ones you're most likely to encounter — along with a few rare breeds worth seeking out.

THE BRITISH NATIVE PONIES

Great Britain probably boasts a larger concentration of pony breeds than anywhere else in the world. Nine distinct breeds have been recognized there for hundreds of years — and two more rare varieties, the Eriskay pony and the Kerry Bog pony, have recently been added to the list, to bring the total to eleven. Though they arose in different parts of the United Kingdom, all of the British native breeds share a common history of survival in an inhospitable climate that today has leant them toughness, stamina, surefootedness, and the ability to survive on very poor forage. These ponies are among the best-known breeds in the world, and they enjoy such popularity that they are now exported and bred on a global basis.

Ponies come in all shapes and sizes. From left: a Gotlund, Fjord, and Haflinger.

THE CONNEMARA

The mountainous, barren terrain of Connemara, in western Ireland, is the home of Ireland's famous indigenous pony. Ancient Celts are thought to have first brought ponies to the Emerald Isle some 2,500 years ago, and it is thought that some Arabian and Thoroughbred blood was introduced to the native stock in the 1700s to lend it refinement (a development that is reflected today in the dished profiles of some Connemaras). The Connemara Pony Breeders Society was formed in 1924 to protect the ponies from indiscriminate breeding and preserve the purity of the bloodlines.

Over the centuries, Irish farmers have depended on sturdy Connemara ponies to work from dawn till dusk, tilling the land, pulling carts, dragging seaweed from the shores to fertilize the fields, carrying turf from the bogs for the hearth, and toting the family children to Mass on Sunday. As if this weren't enough, they often were used for hunting and racing on days of leisure — so in addition to their hardiness, stamina, and longevity, Connemaras have earned a reputation for being nimble and athletic jumpers.

This tallest of the British native pony breeds (ranging from 13 to 14.2 hands, with some individuals achieving horse size) has produced some outstanding show-jumpers and three-day event ponies that have competed on equal footing with horses almost twice their size. A 15-hand Connemara named The Nugget became a puissance champion, clearing a 7'2" barrier at the Olympia Horse Show in London, England, in 1935 — and he was 22 years old at the time. Stroller, Marion Coakes' famous 14.1-hand show-jumping wonder, who won a silver medal at the 1968 Olympic Games, was a half-bred Connemara — and more recently, the Connemara stallion Erin Go Bragh, piloted by Carol Koslowski, was one of the toughest competitors at the Advanced level of three-day eventing in the United States in the 1990s.

Connemaras are most commonly dun or gray, but they also can be black, bay, chestnut, palomino, or any other solid color. They are blessed with an excellent sloping shoulder, which gives them a stride much longer and less choppy than most pony breeds, and short, dense cannon bones, which lend them soundness. Renowned for their versatility in many disciplines, Connemaras are also known for their sensible and willing dispositions. Their popularity with both children and adults has extended worldwide, and there are now Connemara Pony Societies established in at least 17 countries on four continents.

THE EXMOOR PONY

In contrast with the Connemara, the Exmoor pony was on the verge of becoming extinct only a few short decades ago. Fortunately, this living historical artifact is now responding to concerted breeding efforts, and its numbers are rebounding. It is thought that the Exmoor, with its "primitive" coloration and characteristics, represents the closest living link to the ancient wild ponies that roamed Great Britain over 60,000 years ago; fossil records of these ancestral equines do bear a striking resemblance to the modern Exmoor pony with its oatmeal-toned ("mealy") muzzle.

Exmoor is a remote area in the southwest of England known for its bleak, windswept moors and its miserably wet, cold winters. The ponies that roam this area have been molded by natural selection for survival despite the elements. Exmoor ponies have an unusual double-layered winter coat, which provides both insulation and waterproofing, and they also are equipped with a "snow-chute," a patch of short, coarse hairs at the top of the tail that is designed to channel rain and snow away from the body. A unique feature of the breed is the "toad eye," an unusually heavy upper brow that helps protect the pony's eyes from wind and driving rain. Relatively tiny, Exmoors stand no more than 12.3 hands and weigh, on average, about 700 pounds.

In color they are virtually identical, shades of brown or bay being the only acceptable coat pattern, with an oatmeal-shaded muzzle, a light ring around the eyes, and sometimes a buff-colored belly. Their coloring, which helps them blend in well against their natural background of heather, grasses, and bracken, aids them even today, for a few hundred native Exmoors still roam a designated portion of the moors through much of the year. Each fall they are gathered for inspection and branding; only foals that exhibit appropriate coloring and conformation earn the four-pointed star brand of the Exmoor Pony Society.

The population of Exmoor ponies was devastated during World War II when they were neglected, used to feed starving British families, and used in army training as target practice. By 1945 there were only about 50 purebred Exmoors left, and they remain a rare breed with only about 1,200 individuals worldwide.

THE DALES PONY

Native to the eastern slopes of the Yorkshire Dales of James Herriot fame, Dales ponies were originally bred as pack ponies to carry lead from the mines (which were in operation from Roman times up until the mid-19th Century) to the eastern ports, some 250 miles distant. Traveling up to 50 miles a day over rocky terrain, these tough little workers would tote over 100 pounds of lead and ore in one direction then return to the mines loaded up with coal for fuel. In addition to their draft duties, Dales ponies were (and are) known for their comfortable riding gaits and good jumping abilities. The Dales' fast, flashy trot also gave Yorkshire farmers some racing sport on weekends. That trot still serves him well in harness today.

Like the Exmoor, the Dales pony was nearly brought to extinction during World War II. Their compact size made them easier to ship to the European front than larger draft horses. They were put to work hauling artillery, munitions, and supplies. Those ponies that weren't killed in action were left behind at the end of the war to end up on the tables of starving Europeans. The work of a few dedicated individuals has brought the Dales pony back from the edge of oblivion. With the help of a strict breeding program that emphasizes the purity of the breed, they are gaining in popularity once more.

Dales ponies stand up to 14.2 hands, and are predominately black but also may be brown, gray, or bay. White markings are only permitted on the hind legs, as far up as the fetlocks; a small star or snip on the face is also allowed, but too much white is taken as a sign of less-than-purebred status. They are renowned for their hard, well-shaped feet and their powerful, ground-covering stride at the trot. Most sport considerable "feather," the silky straight hair that grows around the hooves. Dales ponies are long-lived and full of pony personality, and their versatility at many tasks has earned them the nickname, "the Great All-Rounder."

THE FELL PONY

Born and bred in the north of England among the hills, or "fells," the Fell pony can trace its ancestry all the way back to horses imported by the invading Romans around 55 BC. He is a close relation of the Dales pony, but has been influenced by the infusion of imported Friesian blood (a high-stepping Dutch carriage horse) as well as some Clydesdale, introduced about 100 years ago. As a result, the Fell pony resembles a miniature Friesian, with snappy knee action at the trot and a proud, high-headed bearing. Like his cousin the Dales pony, the Fell has been used to pack lead ore from the mines to the seaports, and centuries prior to that, he was likely instrumental in the building of the Roman walls that still dot the British landscape. Today he's much in demand as a driving pony and is also popular for pony-trekking, where his surefootedness and ability to carry weight make him suitable for even fairly large adult riders.

Most Fells are solid black and stand between 13 and 14 hands. They sport a well laid-back, sloping shoulder that contributes to their trotting action; a thick, flowing mane and tail; tough hooves with the characteristic "blue" horn(tough hooves so black they look blue), and feathering around the feet.

THE DARTMOOR PONY

The rocky, barren moorland called Dartmoor, near Devon in the southwest of England, is the home of the Dartmoor pony. We know he has existed there for at least a millennium, for reference is made to Dartmoor ponies in the will of a Saxon bishop, Aelfwold of Crediton, in 1012. Used for packing tin from the local mines to the surrounding towns, many Dartmoors were turned loose to roam the moors when not in service. This practice continues today with fenced portions of the moor (called Newtakes) protected by the National Park Authority made available for local farmers to turn their approved mares out with registered Dartmoor stallions. It is thought that this program, which has been in place since 1988, will both help broaden the genetic pool available to breeders and give tourists a chance to see purebred Dartmoors flourishing in their native environment.

Dartmoors remain a rare breed with only about 7,000 individuals in existence, approximately 200 of which are in the United States. They are a small pony with a height not exceeding 12.2 hands, and may be bay, brown, gray, chestnut, or roan. Otherwise, conformationally they are similar to their close cousins, the Exmoors, and their calm dispositions make them ideal children's ponies.

THE NEW FOREST PONY

Named for the forest in southern England where they originated, New Forest ponies occupy one of the largest areas of unenclosed land in the United Kingdom and roam its heaths, woodlands, and bogs as they have for centuries. (They are mentioned in the Domesday Book of 1085.) Narrower in build and swifter of foot than many of the other British-native ponies, it is thought that the New Forest pony has felt the influence of many different infusions of blood from non-pony breeds, such as the Thoroughbred and Arabian. Attempts to standardize the breed only really began in 1906, and outside blood has been prohibited since the mid-1930s.

The ponies that roam the New Forest are privately owned today but essentially are wild; their owners pay for grazing rights in the forest Once a year the ponies are rounded up and evaluated for breeding by the New Forest Pony Breeding and Cattle Society. Despite limited handling, most New Forests show little fear of humans; in fact, it's not uncommon in the autumn months to see ponies wandering casually through the streets of the local towns, intoxicated from eating dozens of fermented acorns!

New Forests are nimble, quick ponies that are much in demand for gymkhana events and mounted games, as well as children's jumper classes; they also excel at long-distance riding. Pony races are a long-standing tradition in the area, and New Forests are surprisingly fast, especially over rough terrain. They range from 12 to 14.2 hands, and may be any solid color with limited white markings on the head and legs.

THE HIGHLAND PONY AND THE ERISKAY

It is not certain whether wild ponies first spread into Scotland after the retreat of the last Ice Age 10,000 years ago, or if they were brought with prehistoric settlers; but fossil records tell us ponies were present in Scottish hills by at least the Eighth Century BC. The ancestors of today's Highland pony carried the Picts across the eastern and northern countryside in 600 AD and have been depicted in primitive art from the era.

Because of the isolation of the highland glens and islands in the 18th and 19th centuries, many sub-types of Highland ponies arose, including the Islay, Rhum, Mull, and Barra strains. The Eriskay pony, a very rare pony found on the Hebrides Islands off the western coast of Scotland, is also thought to be a smaller and lighter strain of Highland pony that has strayed from the original gene pool through long isolation. (Eriskays, which are almost always gray, were long used by Hebridean islanders to carry peat and seaweed in panniers slung across their backs; their docile temperaments made them ideal "back door ponies." Efforts are now being made to revive the breed, which is nearly extinct.)

Traditionally, the Highland pony (or Garron, in Gaelic) was the all-purpose farmer's companion that did all of the work on the crofts (small farms) in the highlands. Before the coming of good roads, sturdy Highland ponies were the main means of transport and served to pack wild game off the hills, including full-sized deer. They excel in carrying the heaviest loads over the roughest and steepest ground with a surefootedness that is remarkable. Today, their quiet nature and weight-carrying ability make them particularly popular for pony trekking (long-distance trail riding, often for tourists).

Highlands range from about 13 to 14.2 hands, occasionally a little larger. They are heavily built, ranging up to 550 kilograms(1,300 pounds) in weight, which makes them the largest of the British native ponies. They often are crossed with Thoroughbreds to produce a horse with more substance and "bone," and a sensible temperament. Interestingly, nearly all Highland ponies are born with "primitive" markings — an "eel" stripe along the spine and faint stripes on the shoulders and legs — that usually fade as they mature. They are the only British native ponies in which these markings occur so frequently, and their appearance suggests an ancient origin.

THE SHETLAND PONY

Familiar the world over, the tiny Shetland is the smallest, and the shaggiest, of the British native ponies. The windswept Shetland Islands, off the northern coast of Scotland, are virtually barren, with no trees, very poor grazing, and a frigid, wet climate. Humans and horses have scraped out a living there for centuries, but no one is sure how or when the Shetland pony first arrived. It seems likely that the Vikings, who settled (or invaded, depending on your view of history) the islands in the first millennium AD, brought their ponies with them, and over the centuries the unwelcoming climate shaped a pony that was built to conserve body heat, with short legs, a stocky body, a thick neck, tiny ears, a remarkably thick mane and tail, and a heavy, water-repellent winter coat. Many Shetlands today also exhibit a dished facial profile, which suggests the influence of some Asian bloodlines somewhere along the way.

For centuries, Shetland islanders depended on their ponies to help bring peat in from the bogs for fuel, to drag seaweed from the shore to fertilize the stony fields, and even to contribute their tail hair for fishing nets. In 1847, when the Mines Act banned children from working in the mines of Great Britain, hundreds of Shetland ponies were pressed into service in their stead. Their small stature (not more than 10.2 hands) meant that they could travel into the narrow underground shafts where a larger pony could not fit. "Pit ponies" often spent years working underground, moving loads of coal and ore, and rarely saw the light of day until their retirement. Though the majority were well cared for, it was a harsh and unnatural existence. Shetlands continued to work in England's mines right up until the 1970s, long after mechanization had made most of their work obsolete.

Today's Shetland is probably the strongest equine in the world relative to its size; even individuals under 10 hands in height are quite capable of carrying a full-grown man or pulling substantial weight in harness. His intelligence and inquisitive, "naughty" temperament are legendary, occasionally making him a challenge to train, though he is also gentle enough to carry tiny children with care. The Shetland comes in almost every color, including pinto, and his thick mane and tail are a trademark of the breed.

THE WELSH PONY

From the hills and valleys of Wales hails the Welsh pony, arguably the most popular pony breed in the world. His history there dates back at least 2,000 years, and there are ample references to him in medieval Welsh literature. Like many other of the British native pony breeds, he roamed wild through the rugged countryside for centuries with little interference from man, although at some point (likely several hundred years ago), a couple of Arabian stallions were turned loose with the herds. Their influence can still be seen in the dished profiles and flowing movement of modern-day Welsh ponies.

The future of the Welsh pony was threatened in the 16th Century, when King Henry VIII decreed that all horses in the British Isles under 15 hands be destroyed because they were not considered useful for warfare. Luckily, because the ponies lived in remote, desolate areas where the king's servants were reluctant or unable to go, they were never discovered, and so continued to flourish.

The Welsh is really four ponies in one, for his registry is divided into four separate sections, labeled A through D. The Welsh Mountain pony (Section A) is considered the ancestral pony, standing 12 hands tall or less, and possessed of a delicate beauty. The Welsh pony (Section B) is a slightly larger version, standing up to 13.2 hands, which was arrived at by careful infusions of Thoroughbred and Hackney blood. The Welsh Pony of Cob Type (Section C) also has a height limit of 13.2 hands, but is a heavier, stockier pony, and the Welsh Cob (Section D) is frequently horse-sized, standing up to 15.2 hands and showing the definite influence of Andalusian blood in his past. All four types of Welsh, and particularly the Welsh Cob, are much in demand as driving ponies, and they are also clever and nimble jumpers. They have large, luminous eyes, an Arabian-type dished face, and may be any solid color, though grays are particularly common.

THE HACKNEY PONY

Though not considered one of the mountain and moorland ponies, the origins of the Hackney pony are undeniably British. He is a dynamic high-stepper developed by crossing the Hackney horse — itself evolving in the early 18th Century as a stylish carriage horse — with small, spirited Welsh ponies. One of the foundation stallions of the Hackney pony breed was a small Hackney named Sir George, foaled in 1866. By the late 1800s, Hackneys were being imported to the United States from England, and it was there that breeders began to make a concerted effort to establish the pony type; today, Hackney ponies outnumber Hackney horses worldwide by 20 to one.

It is thought that the word "Hackney" is a corruption of the French word *hacquenee*, which is derived from the Latin word for horse, *equus*. The term was brought to England by the Normans in the 11th Century, and originally meant a riding horse (as distinguished from the heavier warhorse); our modern term "hack" is an abbreviation. Today, Hackneys are rarely ridden, though many of the ponies are remarkable jumpers. They are almost exclusively found in the show ring, in harness. They have extremely high action both in front and behind, and at the trot, which is performed with piston-like quickness; there is a characteristic moment of suspension when the legs are at their highest point. In temperament, Hackney ponies can be quite "hot" and excitable, a trait that makes them eye-catching in the show ring but largely unsuitable as children's ponies. North American ponies are often shown with their tails docked to a length of a few inches, a practice that is now illegal in Great Britain.

NORTH AMERICAN BREEDS

As native horses inexplicably disappeared from North America thousands of years ago, all of the equines currently in existence on the continent have been imported or are the descendants of imported horses. In the past 200 years, North Americans have not only enthusiastically embraced ponies of breeds from around the world, they have created numerous breeds of their own — whether deliberately or through the will of Mother Nature. Some, like the American Walking Pony, the Trottingbred, and the Quarter Pony, are pony-sized versions of existing horse breeds. Others are complicated mixtures or happy accidents. Here are a few of the more well-known:

THE PONY OF THE AMERICAS (POA)

This versatile Appaloosa-spotted breed is a very recent innovation. It was begun in 1954, when an Iowa breeder named Les Boomhower set out to create an all-round Western-type pony for young riders, based on his foundation stallion, Black Hand. The Appaloosa's influence is the most obvious in this sturdy breed, but POAs also carry the blood of the Arabian, Quarter Horse, and Shetland and Welsh ponies. Black Hand, who was white with what looked like black paint smears on his coat (including a hand-shaped marking on his flank) was sired by a Shetland, out of an Appaloosa/Arab-cross mare.

Boomhower's idea caught on quickly; by 1970 there were

over 12,000 registered POAs, and as of 1995, that number had grown to 45,000. In many ways the POA resembles a small horse rather than a pony. Though he has a height limit of 14 hands, he sports a neat, small head that often demonstrates the Arabian influence; he is heavily muscled, like a Quarter Horse, and his Appaloosa coloring has to be obvious enough to be noticeable from 40 feet away. (These coat patterns may change with the seasons in some ponies.) Most important, because he is bred specifically to be a child's pony, is his calm and easygoing temperament. He is shown almost exclusively by the under-18 set, in events as diverse as barrel racing, bareback jumping, and native costume.

THE CHINCOTEAGUE PONY

Made famous by Marguerite Henry's beloved children's book, *Misty of Chincoteague*, the Chincoteague pony is a feral breed that evolved on the narrow sandbar islands of Chincoteague (pronounced Shin-ko-teeg) and Assateague, off the coast of Maryland and Virginia. Legend has it that they are the descendants of a 16th-Century Spanish galleon shipwreck, but their origins are probably somewhat less romantic than that. There is evidence that 17th-Century mainland farmers turned their horses out on the islands to avoid the payment of livestock tariffs. Natural selection over the centuries has stunted these ponies to an average size of 12 to 13 hands and given them the wiles to survive on these windswept shoals where the salt grasses are tough and fresh water can only be found by pawing in the sand.

The barrier island of Assateague is only 37 miles long and a scant few miles wide, so it can only support a limited pony population. Hence the long-standing tradition of "Pony Penning," in which the feral herds are rounded up, swum across the narrow channel between the two islands, and selected ponies are sold at auction (after which they adapt to a domestic lifestyle quickly, as a rule). Today, Pony Penning is an annual event on Chincoteague, held on the last Wednesday and Thursday of July. Not only does it offer an opportunity to thin the herd (mostly of foals and yearlings), it also gives Virginia state officials a chance to vaccinate and de-worm the animals slated to return to Assateague and attend to other veterinary concerns.

Because the Chincoteague pony is likely a combination of many breeds, his conformation tends to vary, with Arabian and/or Welsh characteristics dominant. Hardiness is his most visible trait, and he is often pinto in coloration.

There are a number of other pony populations on tiny islands scattered along North America's East Coast, including the Banker ponies of Shackleford Island and the Outer Banks of North Carolina, and the Sable Island ponies, which inhabit a sandbar out in the Atlantic, 120 miles east of Nova Scotia They share similar traits — small size, extreme hardiness, an ability to subsist on extremely poor forage with a high salt content, and thick, unruly manes and tails that help protect them from the elements.

THE NEWFOUNDLAND PONY

Early settlers to the somewhat forbidding island of Newfoundland, on Canada's East Coast, brought with them sturdy ponies to help them tame the landscape There is evidence that Exmoor, Dartmoor, Welsh Mountain, Fell, Highland, and Connemara ponies have all had a presence on the island, and their bloodlines became intermingled to eventually produce the Newfoundland pony, well-suited for the harsh environment. An integral part of the island way of life, right up until the 1950s, Newfoundland ponies skidded timbers, hauled firewood, carried kelp for fertilizer, and moved rocks for the farmers and fishermen, and when they weren't needed, they were turned loose to fend for themselves.

Mechanization was slow to come to Newfoundland, but when it finally arrived the pony population plummeted. In desperation, owners, barely surviving on what they scraped from the land and the sea, sold their ponies for meat to

Belgium or France. A government program encouraging the gelding of all young male ponies also proved to be misguided. In 1997 there were only 144 known Newfoundland ponies in all the world and a sizable number of those were geldings and aged mares. Finally, the provincial government of Newfoundland took action, declaring the breed a Heritage Animal and enacting measures for registering, protecting, and promoting the Newfoundland Pony. Since then, the breed's numbers have been steadily climbing with the help of some dedicated breeders, both in Newfoundland and elsewhere in North America.

Newfoundland ponies may be anywhere between 11 and 14.2 hands, and any color, though dark bay predominates. A steady, willing temperament, and an ability to grow plump on the most meager forage, are constants.

THE AMERICAN SHETLAND

The addition of Hackney pony blood to tiny, round Shetland ponies has resulted in a lively, streamlined little animal with a high-stepping action similar to the Hackney The American Shetland is miles away in terms of movement and temperament from his cousins in the north Atlantic; he is a miniature show-ring peacock with refined features and a much finer mane and tail. Like the Hackney pony, he is often shown in harness with exaggeratedly long hooves that enhance his flashy action, though, unlike the Hackney, he retains his long tail.

AND A FEW OTHERS FROM AROUND THE GLOBE...

Almost every country around the world has at least one native pony breed. Many are known only in their native regions, but some have achieved popularity far beyond their borders.

THE HAFLINGER

The Tyrolean Alps of Austria are the ancestral home of this

pretty chestnut pony with the thick flaxen mane and tail. Built like a miniature draft horse, the Haflinger (named for the village of Hafling, originally in Austria, but since World War I, part of Italy) was for centuries the only reliable means of transportation for the local inhabitants. He negotiated narrow paths through the mountains, bearing loads, carrying riders, and sometimes pulling a cart or sled when the roadway was wide enough. Living as part of the family of the mountain peasants, he developed a gregarious and forgiving temperament, which is one of his most prized characteristics today.

All modern Haflingers trace their ancestry to a half-Arabian stallion named 249 Folie, who was foaled in 1874 The Arabian influence is still seen in the refined profiles of the breed They have surprising strength and athleticism for their size (between 13.2 and 14.3 hands) and are much in demand as light draft and harness animals, though they also show talent under saddle. Haflingers are always chestnut (ranging from light sorrel through a chocolate shade) with a lighter mane and tail They are stocky, short-legged, and have wide barrels, giving an overall impression of power without coarseness.

THE GOTLAND PONY

Gotland, an island of wooded moors off the coast of Sweden, is another location where an isolated population of horses has evolved with little intervention from man. Archaeological evidence suggests that the Gotland pony has existed here since the Stone Age, and some researchers suspect he represents the closest living link with the wild Tarpan To this day he exhibits many "primitive" characteristics (including a dun-colored coat with a dorsal stripe), much like Britain's Exmoor.

At the beginning of the 20th Century, increasing settlement of Gotland, with the land-clearing and fences that tend to come with it, had decimated the population of free-ranging Gotland ponies. By World War I they were near extinction, but a few farmers rallied to save them by fencing a large parcel of land for them to run on. A little herd of eight ponies soon began to multiply, and their descendants formed the basis of the breeding stock for the modern-day Gotland. Today there are about 9,000 Gotland ponies in Sweden, Denmark, and Finland, and they have recently begun to attract interest in North America.

Gotlands are relatively tiny ponies, standing only 11.1 hands to 12.3 hands. They are popular as kids' ponies and also are known as swift trotters. (In Sweden, they are often raced.)

THE ASTURIAN

A breed originating in northern Spain, the Asturian (also known as the Asturcon) is a "gaited" pony — that is, instead of trotting, he moves his legs laterally in an ambling gait that is much prized for its smoothness. The gait is an indication of the antiquity of the breed's origins, since horses that moved this way were particularly popular during the Middle Ages as ladies' mounts.

A small pony (averaging 11.2 to 12.2 hands), the Asturian is most often black or bay with no white markings. He sometimes has a rather coarse head, placed on a long, thin neck with a flowing mane. He is officially listed as a rare breed.

THE BASUTO PONY

A descendant of Arabian, Thoroughbred, and Barb horses brought by Dutch settlers to southern Africa in the early 1800s, Basuto ponies are found in modern-day Lesotho, a tiny mountainous nation wholly surrounded by South Africa. Harsh conditions have stunted the pony, but despite his small stature, he is capable of carrying an adult rider for great distances at high altitudes. He averages 14 to 14.2 hands and conformationally resembles his Asian ancestors, with a slender build and prominent withers. Some Basuto ponies are multi-gaited.

In addition to all of these pony breeds (and many we haven't been able to mention here), there are also a number of horse breeds that frequently produce pony-sized individuals. We'll take a look at some of these in the next chapter.

CHAPTER 3

Pony-Sized Horses

In addition to the hundreds of breeds of true ponies, there are also many breeds of horses that regularly produce pony-sized individuals (14.2 hands or under). For the purposes of the show-ring, these animals may be designated as ponies; in some disciplines, this means that they may be shown only by junior exhibitors (those 18 years of age, or younger). Other breeds, descended from full-sized equines, continue to be called horses despite being pony-sized. Here's a representative sampling:

THE ARABIAN

Of all the breeds of horses in the world, it is believed that there is none as beautiful, as pure, or as ancient as the Arabian. His exact origins are lost in the shifting sands of time, but we know that he has inhabited the deserts of Africa and Arabia for more than 4,000 years. The Bedouin people not only considered their Arabians transportation, but also prized members of their family, and often welcomed their horses to sleep in their tents at night. Mares were the favored mounts of the Bedouin warriors, being considered the wisest and most courageous (and less likely than stallions to become distracted by other horses).

Arabians are still noted for their extraordinary stamina and

The Arabian is believed to be the purest equine breed.

toughness, qualities that helped them survive in the desert. Equipped with unusually hard hoof horn, dense "bone" that makes them unusually sound without looking coarse, and black skin that resists the sun's harsh rays, they excel today in long-distance competitive riding, the ultimate stamina test, as well as a multitude of other equine sports. The Arabian has had an influence on virtually every other breed of light horse in the world and more than a few pony breeds as well (the Welsh, in particular).

In addition to his characteristically "dished" face, the Arabian can be identified by his gracefully arched neck, his short back, and the way he carries his tail high, like a flag. He is small, ranging between 14 and 15.2 hands in height. Gray is a predominant color, but Arabians also can be bay, chestnut, roan, and, rarely, solid black (which is much prized).

THE ICELANDIC HORSE

Out on the isolated, windswept, volcanic island of Iceland, hundreds of kilometers from everywhere else in the north Atlantic Ocean, live the descendants of the horses the Vikings rode when they settled the island in 981 AD. Not only is the

Icelandic breed ancient, it's also one of the purest in the world because no other horses have been imported to Iceland for over a thousand years.

The Vikings knew how important horses were to their survival in Iceland and revered them in their mythology. Several Norse gods in the stories owned horses; the most famous was Sleipnir, a magical pacing horse with eight legs. When a Viking warrior died in battle, he often would be buried alongside his best mount. Today, horses remain an important part of Icelandic culture, and there are an estimated 80,000 horses on the island (impressive when you consider the human population is only about 270,000).

The harsh environment of Iceland has produced an extremely sturdy little animal, pony-sized (between 12 and 14 hands) but still referred to by his devotees as a horse. Icelandic horses have dense coats and long, shaggy manes and tails to protect them from the cold, and can survive on very little feed. Although Iceland has no natural predators, the environment itself can be dangerous. There are volcanic eruptions, rock slides, quicksand, and rivers with changing currents to contend with, not to mention a bitterly long and cold winter. Only the wiliest horses survive in such a landscape, and to this day, Icelandic horses have a reputation for not being "spooky" about frightening situations. They also are extremely sure-footed and strong, and despite their small size have no trouble carrying large adults.

The most remarkable thing about the Icelandic horse, however, is the number of ways in which he can move his legs. In addition to

Icelandics can carry adults easily.

performing the normal gaits of walk, trot, and canter, Icelandic horses also pace, and some do a unique gait called the tölt, which is extremely comfortable for the rider and covers a surprising amount of ground (a tölting horse can keep up with another that is galloping!). Icelandic laws continue to keep the breed pure even today — once an Icelandic horse leaves the island he can never return. Exporting horses to other countries is now one of Iceland's biggest businesses, as Icelandics are in huge demand both in North America and Europe. There are more than 100,000 of these horses living outside Iceland now, and they continue to grow in popularity. They come in a multitude of colors, including pinto, and have loving and gentle natures.

THE NORWEGIAN FJORD

Considered a very old and pure breed, the Norwegian Fjord bears a striking resemblance to the horses painted on cave walls by Ice Age artists more than 30,000 years ago. He has been domesticated for more than 4,000 years and was favored by the Vikings as a war mount. Present-day Fjords retain many of the characteristics of primitive Asian wild horses, from which they are thought to have descended, including a distinctive dun coat (ranging from pale cream to brown dun), a dorsal stripe, and zebra markings on the legs. Many also sport a dark cross over the withers, similar to that worn by donkeys. The mane of the Fjord is also unique: the center hairs are dark, and the outer hair on either side is white. Fjord enthusiasts cut the mane short in a traditional crescent shape so it will stand upright. They then trim the outer hairs slightly shorter than the inner dark hairs so that the dramatic dark stripe is displayed.

Fjords are considered draft ponies, standing 13 to 15 hands in height and being broad and muscular in build (weighing an average of 900-1,200 pounds). Their heads, however, are refined and often slightly dished in profile, suggesting the influence of some long-ago Arabian blood. Fjords are known for their gentle, people-oriented personalities and their seemingly endless appetite for work. In Norway and throughout Scandinavia, they are popular for both riding and driving, and often serve as all-around family horses.

THE MORGAN

The Morgan holds the distinction of being the oldest purely American breed of horse, and it is also one of the few to be founded on the influence of a single sire: a little bay stallion, of uncertain origin, named after his owner, Justin Morgan. Morgan, a schoolteacher in colonial Vermont, was given the yearling colt (originally called Figure) in 1789 as partial payment for a debt. Figure matured to a height of only 14 hands but soon became a local legend. He worked long, hard hours in the fields without complaint, he pulled tree stumps better than 2,000-pound draft horses, and he won races against horses nearly twice

The Morgan.

his size. And as a breeding stallion, Figure really shone, for regardless of the kind of mare he bred, the foal was a carbon copy of his sire.

Versatility is the Morgan's trademark even today. He is the ideal family horse, equally adept under English or Western tack or in harness. Not only are Morgans hard workers and easy keepers, staying round and plump on very little feed, but they're also hardy, long-lived, gentle, and flashy-looking. They sport proud, often cresty necks and high knee and hock action. They have been an influence on several other

American horse breeds, including the Saddlebred, Standardbred, Tennessee Walking Horse, and Quarter Horse.

The present-day Morgan differs little from his famous ancestor — he's small (averaging 14 to 15.2 hands) and tends to be bay, brown, or chestnut, though occasionally a buckskin, Palomino, black, or gray Morgan appears. He's stocky in build with a short back, powerful hindquarters, deep barrel, and a neck set high on his shoulders. The Morab, which is a Morgan/Arabian cross, also is frequently pony-sized and is a popular mount for children.

THE PASO FINO

Possessed of a gait so smooth that you can carry a glass of water on horseback and never spill a drop, the Paso Fino has been bred in Latin America since the Conquistadors invaded in the 1500s. A mixture of three fine European breeds — the Andalusian, the Spanish Barb, and the now extinct Spanish Jennet — the Paso Fino first arrived in Santo Domingo

The Paso Fino.

(now the Dominican Republic) with Columbus' second voyage to the New World. Other voyages would add to their numbers in Mexico and South America, and they soon came to be known as "Los Caballos de Paso Fino," the horses with the fine step.

Fancy footwork is the Paso Fino's claim to fame. He walks and gallops just like most of his equine brethren, but instead of trotting, he has a single-footed gait all his own, with footfalls in the same sequence as in the walk, but totally even in cadence. When it's done slowly with collection, it is called a Classic Fino; pick up the pace a little, and it's called a Paso Corto (the best ground-covering, trail-riding gait); and with maximum speed and extension, it's a Paso Largo. The tempo is important; in the show ring Paso Finos are sometimes ridden over a "fino board," a large piece of plywood laid flat on the ground. As the horse moves over the board, the judge will listen for the rhythm and regularity of the footfalls as his hooves tap on the wood. The best are as regular as a metronome.

Paso Finos are small (between 13.2 and 15.2 hands in height, with an average of 14 hands) but dramatic to watch, with a special energy and fire that the Spanish call "brio." They come in every equine color of the rainbow, including palomino, buckskin, and pinto. Paso Finos can be shown in English or Western tack, or in their traditional Spanish gear, and are popular both for children and for older persons who don't want to be bumped around by a trotting horse. Because the ride they give is so smooth, they are also an ideal choice for riders who have arthritis or have suffered an injury, and their sensible dispositions make them popular choices for trail riding.

THE QUARTER HORSE

More people own a Quarter Horse than any other breed of horse in the world. At last count, there were more than 3.5 million registered Quarter Horses, and their popularity shows no sign of slowing down. They have even become all the rage in the United Kingdom and in Europe, where interest in Western-style riding is growing.

As a breed, the Quarter Horse has been around for a couple of hundred years. He developed from the tough, stocky

Chickasaw horse, which in turn was a descendant of the Spanish horses that were first brought to the New World in the 1500s. White colonists crossed the little Chickasaw horse with taller Thoroughbreds, and the result was a useful little horse that could do a bit of everything.

One of the early American settlers' favorite sports was getting together for a friendly horse race. The races were usually held on country lanes or roads, which were often only a quarter of a mile long (about 400 meters). The best racehorses were the ones that could explode forward into a gallop from a standing start and sprint to top speed in a fraction of a second. They soon became known as Celebrated American Quarter Mile Running Horses, which was eventually shortened to Quarter Horse. The Thoroughbred might have been faster over a long distance, but for the short sprint, he was left in the dust by the muscular Quarter Horse.

By the early 1800s, the demand for a rugged and willing horse to help conquer the newly explored West gave the Quarter Horse a new job. Hitched to covered wagons or saddled for long-distance riding, Quarter Horses brought the settlers into the western frontier. And they soon demonstrated another talent — a quality called "cow sense." Ranchers with large herds

The **Quarter Horse.**

of cattle found Quarter Horses valuable work partners when it came to rounding up the herd or moving it from place to place. Not only were they smart and powerful, they were level-headed, too, putting in long days' work without complaint.

Though cattlemen continued to breed Quarter Horses for many years, it wasn't until 1940 that the American Quarter Horse Association was formed to help preserve and promote the breed. Soon after, it seemed everyone discovered the Quarter Horse and his popularity grew by leaps and bounds. Infusions of Thoroughbred blood made him a little taller and less stocky, but he has retained the characteristics that make him so unique: a face with a broad forehead and a large, flat jaw, sharp little ears, powerful shoulders and hindquarters, a short back, and a broad, deep chest. His heavy muscling makes him very good at sports that require sprinting speed, such as barrel racing and polo, and he can turn on a dime, which makes him wonderful for working cattle and for western sports. At 14 to 15.3 hands, he's also an accessible size, with pony-sized individuals common in the bloodlines bred for ranch work and cutting, less so for those bred for English disciplines and halter classes.

The miniature horse.

THE MINIATURE HORSE

Finally, a mention to the smallest member of the equine family, the miniature horse. Designed with horse proportions, shrunk down to canine size, minis are the result of a 20th-

Century breeding program that has used mostly tiny individuals of various horse breeds, rather than ponies, to finally achieve an animal no more than 34 inches tall at the withers (the smaller, the better, according to breeders). Minis are too diminutive to be ridden by anyone but the smallest child, but that doesn't mean they are merely pasture ornaments. Enthusiasts show their minis in-hand (similar to a dog being shown on a leash), and they are also capable of pulling a carriage. They come in every conceivable coat pattern, including pinto and Appaloosa-spotted, and in temperament are positively cuddly. However, their unnaturally small proportions do saddle them with some health problems, including difficulty foaling, a higher rate of pregnancy loss than other breeds, dental difficulties, and dwarfism.

CHAPTER 4

Choosing a Pony

For a child learning about the world of horses, the choice of a first equine companion is pivotal. Wisdom, trustworthiness, and the patience of the saints are required of such a horse or pony, so the search needs to be a careful one.

From the point of view of size, ponies and children go together like peanut butter and jelly. A pony's shorter stride, shorter neck — all of his proportions, in fact, seem tailor-made for a kid. Yet many riding instructors prefer to mount young children on older horses rather than ponies, citing their greater trainability and trustworthiness. Ponies, it seems, have gained a reputation for being devious!

Admittedly, not all ponies wear haloes. Not only do they frequently come

Ponies and children — a natural match.

equipped with quick intelligence and lively personalities, but some also end up less thoroughly trained than their larger cousins simply because they are too small for many adults to ride. Finding a trainer of suitable stature and skill, whether teenager or grown-up, can be difficult. The British cartoonist Norman Thelwell made a career out of illustrating cheerfully sinister ponies hell-bent on ditching their diminutive riders in an endless assortment of clever

> ## AT A GLANCE
>
> • Ponies make ideal mounts for children for size and security reasons.
>
> • In Great Britain and elsewhere, ponies often are ridden by adults.
>
> • Choose a pony based on its intended use and rider experience.

ways (all the while peering innocently out from behind their thatched-roof forelocks!). The reputation is not entirely undeserved.

But even the steadiest old horse may not always be the best choice for a child. Along the road to riding proficiency, falls are inevitable — and a fall from a full-sized horse can be far more frightening, and far more likely to cause serious injury, than a tumble from a pony. Older horses may not be inclined to invest any energy in outlandish behaviors, like bucking or rearing, but they can still shy or stumble on occasion, either of which could cause a parting of the ways. (It goes without saying that younger horses, almost without exception, are a poor match for a beginner rider, whatever the size.)

Furthermore, a child is little more than a passenger on a full-sized horse, which is both too tall and too broad for her short limbs. She will find it a daunting task to apply any meaningful leg pressure to a horse's barrel, and her attempts at motivating her mount may end up being rather less than subtle. We've all seen the kicking, flailing child with the jerking hands who's trying without success to communicate, and most of us would agree that such methods really don't encourage good horsemanship.

A pony, on the other hand, is a considerably more user-friendly equine for the pre-pubescent. A child who can look her prospective partner in the eye is far less likely to be intimidated and much more likely to make a friend. And a child who can groom, tack up, and mount a pony by herself will gain worlds of confidence — not to mention the security of being not that far from the ground once in the saddle. Most ponies don't cover so much ground in a single stride that a child will be frightened by the speed, and their proportions make leg aids easier to apply. There's no guarantee, however, that they'll be obeyed! Finally, it has to be said that the cheeky pony personality is, in many cases, a perfect foil for a cheeky child. A worthy adversary and best friend, all in one package!

If you're seeking a mount for a beginner child, an older pony may be the best investment you could make. With the advantage of longevity — it's not unusual for ponies to still be in service under saddle or in harness well into their 30s or even 40s — most ponies do eventually outgrow the worst of their wickedness, and as youthful exuberance gives way to a world of wisdom, they can become marvelous teachers. A quick peek at the pony classes at any hunter show in North America will reveal a squadron of virtuous 20-plus ponies that have literally shown generations of kids the ropes; each year they return to the show ring with a new little student on board. Such animals are indispensable for what they provide in safety, experience, and patience.

Ponies have ease of care in their favor, as well. Not only do they thrive on very little feed, but many never have need of shoes. Hardiness is no excuse for neglect, of course, but if you're looking to keep an equine on a limited budget, ponies are refreshingly thrifty beasts.

PONIES FOR GROWN-UPS

All of these advantages hold true not only for children just entering the world of horses, but also for more experienced horsepeople, both young and old. For ponies aren't just babysitters with thick manes, they're challenging and rewarding equines for adults as well.

North American horse people — well, the adults, anyway — seem to be a bit embarrassed about the idea of riding

In many countries, adults ride ponies.

ponies. Perhaps they fear others thinking they can't handle a full-sized horse (a creature not so nearly as full of guile and cleverness as a pony, as we've noted already). No such problem exists in many other parts of the world, including Great Britain, where ponies are popular mounts for many grown-ups seeking minimum-maintenance, maximum-fun companions for trekking, foxhunting, or even mounted games. It's important to remember that a pony's ability to carry weight is far greater than you'd surmise from his size; even a 10-hand Shetland pony can carry a 200-pound man without breaking a sweat. If you're looking for an all-around family pet, a large pony or cob could fill the bill as mount for both Mom and the kids for a considerable number of years. And unless you are very tall, you will probably find you don't feel at all awkward on a pony; most have broad barrels that can take up quite a length of leg and don't "feel" small once you're on board. And just imagine how much easier mounting would be!

Another way for ponies and adults to enjoy each other is to pursue driving. Many pony breeds excel in harness and compete alongside horses at the highest levels of driving competition. If you really want to develop an appreciation for ponies as athletes, consider the sport of combined driving, where Welsh ponies, Dales, Fells, Haflingers, Fjords,

Connemaras, and many other breeds have proven the value of their surefootedness and extraordinary common sense while being driven at considerable speeds over hill and dale, through streams and forests, and past all sorts of complex questions of terrain. Regardless of your size, driving can provide you with a wonderful way to enjoy a relationship with a pony (or ponies).

CHOOSING THE RIGHT ONE

Identifying the right pony for your needs isn't the simplest task in the world; not only are there a bewildering number of breeds from which to choose (not to mention a great many mixed-breed ponies of various virtues), but you'll also have to consider each individual's conformation, soundness, and temperament.

If you're buying a first pony for your child, you'll want a real "packer" — a pony with a long history of reliability and an age that at least makes him eligible to vote. Worry less about good looks than about safety; often, the plain-brown-wrapper pony turns out to be the real diamond in the rough, the one with the soul of a teacher and the patience of Job. When trustworthiness is the main issue, you may even be able to compromise on some soundness issues. (For example, an older pony may suffer from arthritic joints, but could be made comfortable with the judicious use of anti-inflammatory medications, such as

Suitability is an important consideration.

Bute.) What you don't want to compromise on is solid training; an uneducated pony is in no condition to teach a young rider. In short, you want him "broke to death" and bombproof (two qualities that make even some aged ponies worth quite a bit of money).

Many people entertain the notion of buying a young, "green" pony, and letting it loose with their child so they can "learn together."

Let's be blunt about this approach: It's a recipe for disaster.

Most child riders are far too green themselves to cope with an uneducated pony, and almost invariably the child ends up injured, or at least severely frightened, and gives up on horses altogether. Then the parent is left with a spoiled or frightened pony that will be very difficult to sell because he's no longer so young and has a history of being unsafe with children. Avoid this mistake at all costs, please.

On the other hand, if you are an experienced trainer, you might want to consider taking on a young pony to school and sell as a child's mount later on. Well-trained, reliable ponies are always in demand for riding schools, private homes, and the show ring, and if you like a challenge, you may find that you really enjoy working with ponies. Their intelligence makes them quick studies, but it also provides for a lot of creative, and entertaining, evasions along the way. They certainly should never be underestimated; many a trainer who has begun thinking, "oh, he's only 12 hands high, how much trouble could he be?" has soon developed a healthy respect for the more diminutive equine!

Because good trainers of a suitable size to school ponies are sometimes rare, there are also a great number of poorly-educated, "half-broke" ponies on the market with any number of behavior problems or bad habits. Sometimes they have just been badly frightened; more often, they have been spoiled rotten by well-meaning but ignorant owners and have discovered that a little rudeness will get them out of any amount of work. These little criminals can sometimes be difficult to

Well-trained, reliable ponies are always in demand.

reform, but if you are up to the task, it can be very rewarding to make "solid citizens" of them.

Though there are a couple of pony breeds that are specialists (the high-stepping Hackney pony, for example), the vast majority are successful jacks-of-all-trades. This versatility often means that a single pony can fulfill a whole family's wishes. Imagine, for example, that you are looking for a pony to compete in pleasure driving classes, while your daughter wants to show-jump — a Connemara or Welsh pony (to name only two breeds) could easily fill the bill for both sports. A pony doing double duty will, of course, need to be physically up to both tasks, so more stringent standards may need to be applied in regard to soundness — but the inherent hardiness of most ponies makes this less of an issue than it would be for horses.

If you're new to the world of ponies, it may be worth consulting an expert before you buy. Bloodlines are likely only an issue if you're intending to get into the breeding game, but quirks of conformation, color, or movement could be a consideration if you're planning to show, and they might also have an impact on the pony's long-term usefulness. Above all, though, choose a pony with a disposition suitable for your plans. Novices should always place an emphasis on an honest, kind nature. Ponies of a more fiery temperament should be reserved for those horsepeople with years of experience.

Remember: sometimes the biggest challenges come in small packages!

CHAPTER 5

Pony Health and Maintenance

Ponies are such hardy little animals that their health-care routines are usually quite low maintenance — in stark contrast to many of their larger cousins. If you are used to horses, some of whom are accidents looking for a place to happen, you will be pleasantly surprised by the comparatively few veterinary bills incurred by the average pony. Their common sense and surefootedness keep them out of many scrapes, and on the whole, they tend to be disease-resistant, long-lived, and easy to care for.

That's not to say that a pony's health needs should be ignored. Regular deworming, vaccinations, and attention to the teeth are part of the routine veterinary care every pony and horse is entitled to. Consult with your veterinarian to determine the best schedule of vaccinations and a deworming program that will suit your pony best. Under most circumstances, ponies and horses should be treated with a paste dewormer at least once every three months and vaccinated yearly for tetanus, rabies, and in some cases, Eastern and/or Western equine encephalomyelitis (EEE and WEE). Other vaccines also may be a good idea depending on where you live and what your pony is used for; if you're in the eastern part of North America, you might want to vaccinate against Potomac Horse Fever, for example. If he's travelling to shows on a regular basis and is exposed to many other horses and ponies, you might consider vaccinating him against respiratory diseases like strangles and influenza. (Intra-nasal vaccines, which have far greater efficacy than the older intra-muscular formulations, can protect against both strangles and influenza.) Bear in mind that some vaccines will need to be repeated more than yearly for best protection.

Regular attention to dental care is a must for all ponies; most will need to have the

AT A GLANCE

• Most ponies are low maintenance, but routine health care such as deworming, vaccination, and attention to teeth, is important.

• Obesity and laminitis are two health concerns for ponies. Laminitis can be triggered by a variety of factors, including overeating.

sharp edges of their molars filed down, or "floated," at least once a year. Geriatric equines, in particular, often develop tooth problems, which can seriously compromise their ability to chew and digest their feed. As your pony ages, it's a good idea to increase the frequency of his dental inspections; your veterinarian may not need to take action on every examination, but at least you'll keep on top of any developing problems.

Hoof care shouldn't be neglected, either, even if your pony is barefoot and enjoys a fairly natural outdoor lifestyle. He'll need to have his feet trimmed by a qualified farrier at least once every six to eight weeks. Otherwise, his overgrown feet will tend to split, crack, make him prone to thrush (a fungus infection of the frog and soft foot structures) and stumbling, and eventually put an unhealthy strain on the ligaments and tendons of his legs.

There are a few specific health concerns that seem to surface more frequently in ponies than in their larger kin. Some of these, ironically, are a direct result of a pony's inherent hardiness and ability to survive on the poorest forage: he's rather poorly adapted to the rich feed and limited excrcise of a domestic lifestyle. The combination of these can sometimes overwhelm a pony's system and have devastating consequences. Often, pony owners find they have to be "cruel to be kind" — limiting their pony's access to rich pasture or high-protein hay and resisting the temptation to feed grain. Such steps may seem heartless on the outside (and ponies won't let you forget it!), but they will help ensure your charges' long-term health.

Let's take a look at some of the health problems liable to crop up in ponies.

OBESITY

Because ponies, for the most part, evolved to survive in extreme conditions and on very poor quality forage, they have low metabolic rates and tend to be easy keepers. This makes them very susceptible to obesity. Because they are so round to begin with and often sport long, thick winter coats, it can be easy to overlook a pony's weight gain — but being severely overweight can have long-term health consequences, just as it does for humans. It's a good idea to have your veterinarian evaluate your pony's weight and condition at least once a year. You can also get a reasonable idea of whether he's at a healthy size by running a hand over his barrel; you should be able to feel his ribs when you apply a little gentle pressure, but not see them when you stand back and observe him.

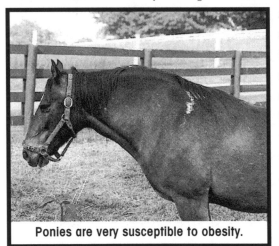

Ponies are very susceptible to obesity.

The cure for obesity, incidentally, is the same as it is for humans — eat less and exercise more. Many ponies get far too little exercise. If yours is baby sitting a young child, for example, and rarely breaks out of a walk when ridden, consider providing him with more of a workout by longeing him for 20 to 30 minutes every day or turn him out in a large field (preferably with sparse grazing — more on the importance of that in a moment).

LAMINITIS

Laminitis, or founder, is a severe and painful condition of the hooves (generally the front ones, though ponies and horses can founder in the hind feet or in all four). It occurs when some sort of insult or injury triggers vascular constriction, which shunts the blood away from the small capillaries and into the larger blood vessels of the leg. When this happens, most of the blood ends up bypassing the feet, and without a steady nutrient supply, the cells of the laminae (the vascular tissues on the interior of the hoof wall, which help attach the hoof to the internal structures like the coffin bone) begin to starve and die. Within hours, the firm Velcro-like connection between the laminae and the hoof wall begins to disintegrate. Without its stabilizing influence, the coffin bone is no longer supported and begins to sink down toward the sole, or rotate, so it's no longer parallel to the hoof wall. Needless to say, the condition is exquisitely painful for the pony, which ends up rooted to the spot, unwilling to take a single step on his inflamed feet. He may stand with his front feet parked out in front of him or rock back on his heels, trying to relieve the pressure. His feet will likely feel warm to the touch, and a digital pulse (detected in a vessel running down the back of the pastern, near the heels) will be clearly noticeable (in a healthy horse, it's hard to find).

Studies have shown that a laminitis episode actually can begin well before the pony shows any obvious signs. Hours before lameness and pain are evident, the laminae already might be losing shape and function. Once the laminae begin to lose their grip on the hoof capsule, a disastrous chain of events is already under way. In the majority of cases, some degree of rotation of the coffin bone is the result, and the greater the differential between the coffin bone's normal position and its rotation, the more severe the laminitis. (Radiographs are used to determine the exact degree.) As it

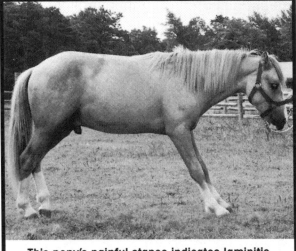

This pony's painful stance indicates laminitis.

rotates, the pointed tip of the coffin bone begins to compress the soft vascular "bed" that lines the hoof's inner sole. This compression can cause severe damage to the complex maze of nerves and vessels that supply nutrients to the hoof's interior structures and can become a major source of continuing pain, long after the initial laminitis attack.

One of the insidious things about laminitis is that the foot may continue to deteriorate long after the episode that first triggered the vascular changes. As tissues continue to die off, the coffin bone may end up in a more and more unnatural position, sometimes sinking right through the bottom of the sole over a period of days or weeks.

In all cases of laminitis, immediate and expert veterinary care is essential; the sooner the process can be detected and treated, the better the prospects for recovery. Anti-inflammatory drugs such as Bute and stall rest are prescribed at first. (The more the horse moves, the greater the number of laminae that may tear away from the hoof wall.) After the initial crisis is past, your veterinarian and farrier should work together to determine the best way to help support your pony's coffin bones and encourage healing. This often requires radical changes in the way his hoof is trimmed, and in most cases, it will require therapeutic shoes. Recovery may be a months-long process, and some severe cases never return to soundness. The affected hooves tend to grow in a concave fashion, curling up somewhat at the toes to give the impression of a Turkish slipper. A pony sporting such feet and a short "stabbing" stride is said to have foundered. What's worse, a foundered pony is forever vulnerable to further attacks, which can create chronic and sometimes severe lameness.

Laminitis is so common in ponies as to be seen as almost endemic. But it doesn't have to be. Careful management can help your pony avoid the perils of founder, a disease in which prevention is a far better prospect than cure! Knowing what is likely to trigger an attack is the best defense. Possible causes may include:

• repeated pounding on hard surfaces (road founder);

• toxemia (the circulation of toxins, either bacterial, viral, or chemical, in the bloodstream) in the aftermath of a severe injury or disease (such as pleurisy, pneumonia, or Potomac Horse Fever);

• in mares, retaining the placenta after foaling;

• increased pressure on one foot as a result of severe lameness in the opposite leg (unilateral laminitis);

• adverse drug reactions (usually to corticosteroids or vaccines);

• Cushing's syndrome, a condition common in older ponies that compromises the immune system and makes them prone to founder (see Chapter Nine for more on Cushing's);

• severe stress, such as long-distance shipping in extremely hot, humid conditions, or undergoing surgery;

• being bedded on shavings containing black walnut; this wood is so toxic to horses it can trigger laminitis just by contact;

• drinking large quantities of water immediately after hard exercise;

• and most commonly, overeating — breaking into the feed

room and gorging on grain, for example, or consuming too much rich spring grass (grass founder).

As we've pointed out above, ponies can easily become obese on the kind of feed we North Americans tend to put in front of our horses. Couple existing obesity with a day out on lush spring grass, and laminitis is practically a predictable result. We're not sure of the exact mechanism by which it happens, but in crude terms the pony's system goes on overload. So as much as you may want to let your pony enjoy nature's bounty, you may do him a great favor by instead limiting his access to rich forages. Turn him out for only an hour or so in the spring, and gradually increase his pasture time as the season lengthens and the grass matures and becomes less rich. The rest of the time, as cruel as it may seem, he may be better off in a dry lot (a paddock without grass). Choose low-protein grass hay for him if he's finished growing, and be very careful about offering grain (most ponies have no need of it unless they are in very hard work).

HYPERLIPEMIA

Hyperlipemia might be considered the flip side of obesity. It's a peculiar condition that can occur in horses, but is much more common in ponies, often beginning when an obese pony suddenly drops a lot of weight.

In hyperlipemia, the body perceives itself to be starving so it releases large quantities of stored lipids (fats) into the bloodstream — generally more than the pony can use. At the same time, the system seems to say 'no more,' and it shuts down the appetite. A pony suffering from hyperlipemia will be feverish, drowsy, or depressed, and might suffer muscle twitching, a lack of coordination, colic, diarrhea, and impaired liver and kidney function. He'll tend to refuse all feed, no matter how tempting.

Hyperlipemia can appear rapidly and has a high fatality rate — and it is difficult to treat because the only cure is to feed a high-energy, low-fat diet for a period of one to three weeks to an animal with little enthusiasm for food. Enticing the pony with beet pulp or chaff (chopped hay or oat straw) with molasses laced with fruit juice, apples, or carrots sometimes does the trick. Some veterinarians administer heparin, an anticoagulant, to help break down the fats already in the bloodstream. Giving insulin and/or glucose has also been investigated as a means of keeping the body from releasing more fats into the blood.

We don't yet fully understand what triggers hyperlipemia, but we do know that ponies and miniature horses are particularly vulnerable to it, and that mares that have recently foaled or that are lactating (producing milk) are the highest-risk group. Stress seems to be a factor, which is why sudden, dramatic weight losses pose a risk, as do heavy loads of internal parasites, shipping, and other severe changes in lifestyle. If your pony is obese, aim for a program of gradual weight loss rather than a starvation diet; it will likely have better results anyway.

GERIATRIC COMPLAINTS

Ponies past their mid-teens may suffer from a variety of age-related diseases and problems. For more on these, please see Chapter 9: The Older Pony.

CHAPTER 6

Feeding Your Pony

Many people seem to find the subject of equine nutrition rather bewildering, but it really isn't rocket science. Once you understand a few basic principles, the mysteries of feeding begin to reveal themselves, and you'll find designing a nutritionally complete diet for your pony a relatively straightforward process. Let's start by taking a quick tour of the equine digestive system, so we can see what he is designed to eat — and what he isn't.

THE TUMMY TOUR

Horses and ponies are monogastric (single-stomached) herbivores, designed for a grazing lifestyle. Their natural diet is tough, gritty grasses and other pasture plants, consumed in small quantities over many hours of wandering and nibbling. (In the wild, ponies will graze for 16 to 20 hours every day.) These forage plants are torn off by the pony's sharp incisors, and the grinding of the molars begins to bruise and tear the stringy fibers. Once swallowed, the material makes a one-way journey down the esophagus. (Unlike most animals, horses and ponies cannot vomit, an evolutionary oversight that makes them vulnerable when they ingest a toxic substance; fortunately, they have excellent instincts when it comes to avoiding poisonous plants, so poisoning is rarely a problem.)

Both ponies and horses have surprisingly small stomachs for their size; the organ can only accommodate about two to four gallons (7.5 to 15 liters) of material. As a result, very little breakdown of food particles goes on in the stomach; there are enzymes that do a little bit of digesting and a lot of liquefying of the feed, but within about 15 minutes (or as soon as the stomach reaches about two-thirds of its capacity), everything gets pushed on by muscular contractions to the next stop on

> # AT A GLANCE
>
> • Ponies' stomachs are designed for a grazing lifestyle.
>
> • Nutritionists recommend that ponies be fed between 1.5% and 3% of their body weight in total feed every day.
>
> • Under most conditions, ponies get all the nutrition they need from forage.

the tour: the small intestine, some 60 to 70 feet of coiled, convoluted tubes suspended from the loin region by a fan-shaped membrane called the mesentery. The small intestine can hold up to 30% of the gastrointestinal tract's total capacity, and it's where protein, starches, fats, calcium, phosphorus, and most vitamins are digested. These nutrients pass through the intestinal wall and are carried to the cells throughout the body, either for immediate use or, in some cases, to be stored for future needs. The stuff that isn't absorbed — largely fiber — is pushed on to the large intestine, a journey that takes from 60 to 90 minutes all told.

The large intestine is divided into several sections: the cecum, the large (or ascending) colon, the small colon, and the rectum and anus. The cecum is where the bulk of the hard work of digestion is done — it's a huge fermentation vat where beneficial microbe populations efficiently break down tough plant fibers into simpler compounds called volatile fatty acids (VFAs), which can be absorbed through the gut wall. These plant fibers (largely composed of cellulose and other hard-to-digest molecules) pass through the stomach and small intestine untouched, but the symbiotic bacteria in the cecum make short work of them, usually breaking them down within about five hours.

From the cecum, the partially digested food moves on to the large colon, where fermentation continues for another 36 to 48 hours. By the time the material moves on to the small colon, nearly all of the nutrients the pony's body needs from his meal have been extracted; what's left over is what he cannot digest or use. The main function of the small colon is to reclaim the excess liquid. By the time the material leaves this area, it has become solid again and has been molded into fecal balls. All in all, it takes between 36 and 72 hours for a meal to make the complete journey through the gastrointestinal tract and for the leftovers to be expelled as manure.

Under normal conditions, the equine digestive system functions very well, but it is sensitive to sudden changes in diet or environment. An abrupt change in diet, for example, can alter the internal pH in the cecum and trigger a massive death of the gut microbes, which are essential to fiber digestion. This not only can make it difficult for the pony to extract all the nutrients he needs from the forage portion of his diet, but it may also put him at risk for colic and laminitis.

Horses and ponies are also rather poorly adapted to digesting large amounts of carbohydrates, such as are found in most grains (oats, corn, or barley). This is particularly true of ponies. When a pony ingests a large grain meal, the small intestine may not have time to process all of the carbohydrates before the feed gets pushed on to the cecum. There, trouble brews because the fermentative bacteria in the cecum don't process the carbohydrates well. They try, but a resulting buildup of acids (a byproduct of the fermentative digestion of carbohydrates) lowers the pH level in the hindgut, making the environment hostile for the bacteria, and they begin to die off, releasing toxins as they do so. Again, the stage is set for colic and laminitis. Suddenly, the wisdom of locking the feed room so your ponies cannot break in and gorge on grain becomes clear!

Because ponies evolved to survive (and even thrive) on the

poorest of forages, they really do best when you make an effort to offer them meals that mimic their natural diet. That means fibrous plant material and little or no carbohydrates. Only very fit, highly bred ponies (such as some Hackney ponies or Thoroughbred crosses) being used for high-performance sports are likely to need the concentrated calories of grain to give them extra energy and help them maintain good weight. The vast majority of healthy ponies have no trouble keeping a well-rounded physique on forage (pasture and/or hay) alone.

WHAT AND HOW MUCH TO FEED

As a general rule of thumb, nutritionists recommend that horses and ponies be fed between 1.5% and 3% of their body weight in total feed every day. The range allows you to make dietary adjustments depending on whether the horse or pony needs to gain weight or lose it, or whether the work he is doing requires more or less energy. Because the metabolism of ponies is so efficient, it's a good idea to stick close to the lower range of the 1.5% and 3% formula for them. So for instance, if you had an adult Welsh pony weighing 300 kilograms (approximately 660 pounds), he should consume about 4.5 kilograms (or 9.9 pounds) of feed on a daily basis.

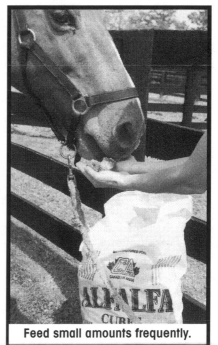

Feed small amounts frequently.

Because ponies are grazing animals, they're designed to take in small amounts of food on an almost-continuous basis. In essence, their hunger signals are always on. In a domestic environment, however, ponies can't always have access to feed when they want it. Often, this results in frustration and chewing of surfaces that aren't a normal part of the diet — fences, stalls, saddles, or whatever might be in reach! What's worse, when we feed ponies according to our own convenience instead of according to their natures, in one or two large meals a day and nothing in-between, we are forcing their digestive systems to work contrary to their design, and the results can be catastrophic. As much as possible, then, it's important to feed your pony small amounts, often, rather than large amounts, infrequently.

Pasture is the cheapest way to provide forage for a pony and also one of the healthiest. If he has space to wander and graze, choosing the plants he likes best and exercising his muscles (not to mention absorbing vitamin D from the sun), you'll be providing him with the closest thing to his natural lifestyle. Although we are often warned against turning ponies out on spring pasture, there's nothing inherently wrong with ponies grazing on this lush forage — it's just that many ponies gorge on its sweetness after a winter of less-appetizing hay, and the sudden dietary change can trigger a major digestive upset, leading to grass founder. If your pony lives outside winter and summer, he'll adapt to the spring growth as it begins to emerge, and you should have no difficulties; if, however, he

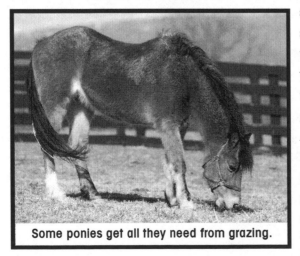
Some ponies get all they need from grazing.

spends his nights in a stall and is fed hay through the winter, you will need to introduce him to spring grazing gradually. Allow him only an hour's worth on the lush growth for the first few days, then over a period of a few weeks increase the amount of time he grazes as the pasture plants get older and less rich. By summer his system will have adjusted, and you will have avoided the risk of founder.

Hay is simply dried pasture grasses, and it's a fine substitute for grazing whenever natural forage is poor (both during the winter and in summer drought conditions, for example). The long stems of baled hay help to satisfy a pony's natural grazing and chewing urge and keep him occupied. Good quality hay should be green and sweet-smelling, not full of large seedheads (they are an indication that the hay was over-mature when cut and will be short on some nutrients, as well as tough to chew), and of course free of dust and mold. The type of hay you choose will depend on the ponies you're feeding. Young growing ponies and breeding stock (mares in their last trimester of pregnancy, mares nursing foals, and stallions being used to cover mares) benefit from the higher protein and calcium levels contained in legume hay (alfalfa and/or clover), while mature animals not being used for breeding do much better on lower-protein grass hay (timothy, brome, orchard grass, or any of a number of other varieties, depending on what part of the world you live in). Mixed hay, which contains some grass and some legume, is an appropriate choice for many adult ponies, too; just be sure that the mix is heavy on the grasses and light on the legumes.

Under most conditions, ponies can extract all the nutrients they need from forage alone; in this respect they are far more efficient digestive machines than horses. To determine exactly what nutrients your hay or pasture is supplying, however, you'll need to test it; a forage analysis can be arranged by your county agricultural extension office or your local feed store. It's an inexpensive way to determine whether your pony's diet is lacking in any essential nutrient; if you find there are deficiencies, you can supplement those with vitamins or minerals.

Young growing ponies need higher levels of certain nutrients — most important, protein, calcium, phosphorus, copper, and zinc — in order to develop strong bones, teeth, hooves, and soft tissues. This need is most acute before their first birthday, when they are growing rapidly, .

As very young foals, they get everything they need from their mother's milk, but as they grow, their digestive systems prepare for the switch to solid food, while their dam's udders become gradually less bountiful. Small quantities of a "creep" ration, based on milk protein and especially designed for growing foals, can be helpful in bridging the gap and ensuring your foal's legs grow straight and strong. They also can help ease the transition at weaning time — but bear in mind the efficient metabolism of most pony breeds and resist the temptation to over-feed. Pony weanlings generally need only a fraction of the feed their larger cousins might require.

Lactating mares are another category with increased nutrient needs; in fact, it's estimated that nursing a growing foal is one of the most strenuous activities a horse or pony can undergo, even more strenuous than the pregnancy. Some mares seem to donate all of their own stored nutrients to their foals and can quickly become bone racks; others are copious milkers and seem to have no trouble maintaining their own weight. Monitor your nursing mares closely while they have foals at foot, and provide them with legume-based hay; add a small amount of a commercial grain ration designed for broodmares if you notice them losing weight. In rare instances, stallions lose weight during breeding season, and they can benefit from a broodmare ration as well.

SALT AND WATER

Whatever the age or the status of your pony, don't forget the other two essential nutrients in his diet: salt and water. Ponies and horses should always have salt available to lick, either loose or in 'brick' form. They'll usually consume only as much as they need. (You can also add some loose salt to their feed, but in moderation.)

A horse or pony can live several days without feed, but dehydration can claim him very quickly. In winter, pay special attention to make sure he always has access to water. Keep outside troughs clear of ice (a submersible heater is the easiest way to accomplish this), break ice that forms in inside buckets, and try to offer lukewarm water a few times a day. (Making sure your pony doesn't get dehydrated in winter can also cut down on the chance he'll develop impaction colic.)

The only time it's wise to restrict a pony's access to water is just after he has exercised hard. Though he may be thirsty then, he can throw his system into shock and develop colic or founder if he takes in large quantities of cold water. While he's cooling down, offer him a few sips of water every few minutes, and only give him free access to water again once he's completely recovered and his pulse is back to a 'resting' rate (under 48 beats per minute).

FEEDING OLDER PONIES

Geriatric ponies (which we'll talk about more thoroughly in Chapter 9) have some special feeding needs, both because their digestive efficiency is compromised and because they often suffer from dental problems that make chewing difficult. In addition, very old ponies frequently suffer from a loss of appetite. So when you design a diet for a senior citizen, you need to consider ease of chewing, the availability of the nutrients in the feed, and good palatability. Instead of stemmy, mature, 100% grass hay, opt for a higher-quality, softer, and less mature mixed hay with a fairly high legume content (up to 60% or so). Your aging equine will find it much easier to chew. As a test, grab a handful of the hay and squeeze hard — if the hay hurts your hand, it's likely too tough and fibrous for your old guy. For most older ponies, it's still a good idea to avoid straight alfalfa hay — while soft and very palatable, it has an excessively high protein content and is very low in phosphorus. (If your pony has a liver or kidney dysfunction, it's particularly important to avoid high-protein legume hays; instead, choose a grass hay that is immature and thus still fairly soft. More on these conditions in Chapter 9.)

There may come a day when even high-quality, soft hay is too much of a chore for your older pony. In this case, you may have to do some of the chewing for him, so to speak. Chopped hay is a good start — you can chop it yourself or buy it already chopped in bagged form. Or you may want to consider one of the great variety of hay cubes or pellets available. Because these tend to be rather hard in texture, soak them in warm water for an hour or two before feeding to make a gruel or a soup.

Soaked sugar beet pulp is still another excellent fiber source for older ponies — it's soft and very easily chewed (suitable for even the most toothless geriatric), extremely digestible, and a good source of calcium. Bran, however, is not a great choice, even though most ponies love the taste of a

Some older ponies need added fat in their diets.

bran mash. It's only a fair fiber source, is relatively indigestible, and has far too high a phosphorus content to be a healthy daily feed.

The decreased efficiency of the digestive tract means that some ponies will need the help of a little grain (which is more calorie-dense than forage) to help maintain their condition in their senior years. A commercial pelleted or extruded ration is usually a better idea than unprocessed whole grains. They are made with finely ground grains, so in a sense they are "pre-chewed." Pelleted feeds, in particular, are easy to soak in water to make a mush for a very old and toothless pony.

The nutritional needs of an aging pony are in many ways similar to those of a weanling, especially in terms of protein

British Native ponies: the Connemara (above) and the Exmoor (below).

Other British Native ponies: the Fell (above); the Shetland (below); the Welsh Mountain (opposite, above); and the Welsh (opposite, below).

The Hackney also has its origins in the British Isles
and is found primarily in the show ring, in harness.

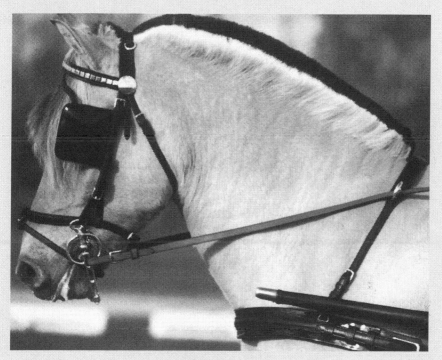

The Norwegian Fjord.

The Newfoundland pony (above) is descended from sturdy ponies brought to the island by early settlers; the Icelandic (below) is pony-sized but considered a horse.

The Haflinger originated in the Tyrolean Alps of Austria.

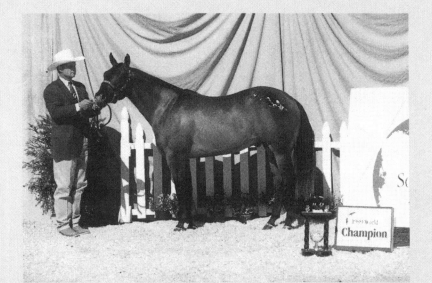

Some American breeds: Pony of the Americas (above) and the Chincoteague (below).

levels, calcium, and phosphorus. So feeds designed for young horses may be a good choice, as are those formulated particularly for older horses. "Senior" feeds are often manufactured with a softer-textured pellet format that improves their palatability; they are justifiably popular with many owners.

Feeds with added fat are also excellent for all older ponies, except for those with liver dysfunction. Fat, in the form of vegetable oils or rice bran, is extremely digestible and can help immeasurably in keeping an older pony's ribs covered as it contains almost two and a half times more energy, pound for pound, than carbohydrates. Adding fat is an excellent way to increase the calorie density of your pony's diet without increasing its volume by more than a few ounces. You can top-dress vegetable oil to a level of up to two cups per day (spread over several meals a day) or choose to buy a feed that is formulated with extra fats (look for a feed tag that lists a crude fat level of at least 5%, and preferably up to 8%). If you feed rice bran, look for a brand that is calcium-supplemented; this will help compensate for its unusually high phosphorus content. (Feeding more phosphorus than calcium can result in a systemic imbalance and, in the long term, brittle and porous bones.)

You may also want to consider adding a probiotic product to your older pony's feed. Probiotics are products designed to help aid digestion; they may be feeds that help keep the microbial populations in the cecum thriving, or they may be actual bacterial cultures that can aid in fermentative digestion. Brewer's yeast is a good and inexpensive probiotic that seems to improve feed utilization (by encouraging the health of the gut microflora) and also is an excellent source of B vitamins, a deficiency of which is a concern particularly for older ponies with pituitary tumors (Cushing's disease) and liver disease.

(To learn more about the principles of feeding, please look for my companion book, *Understanding Equine Nutrition*, also part of the Horse Health Care series.)

CHAPTER 7

Pony Psychology

THE HERD INSTINCT

To really understand what drives the instincts and intellect of a pony, what frightens him, and what motivates him, it's essential to realize that ponies and horses are first and foremost herd animals. As herbivores with few natural weapons against predators, the distant ancestors of today's ponies found safety in numbers. A single pony in the wild is vulnerable; a family group much less so, especially in an environment of open grassland where shelter and hiding places are few and far between. The herd instinct remains the single strongest motivating factor in every horse and pony today, regardless of whether he comes from 2,000 years of domesticated stock or not. In one way or another, it underlies nearly every decision he makes.

A typical family group of wild (or, more correctly, feral) ponies consists of a single stallion, several mares (the exact size of the harem is a tribute to the magnetism and fighting ability of the stallion), and an assortment of foals and juvenile colts that are too young to be considered a threat to the dominant male's authority. (At the age of about two most colts are driven away from the herd by the dominant stallion and either form bachelor groups or acquire their own harems.)

The stallion's role is not only reproductive, but protective as well; he tends to patrol the perimeter of the herd's territory, scenting for danger and taking the brunt of any challenge from a rival stallion. In the day-to-day dealings of the herd, however, a series of complex social hierarchies decides where each individual stands.

Horses and ponies establish a definite pecking order in any group. A pony's rank in the hierarchy depends on a number of factors — age, size, personality (some animals are just naturally more aggressive; others are pacifists), heredity (dominant mares tend to produce dominant foals), and even color, with darker-colored individuals usually dominant over lighter-colored ones, such as duns, grays, or palominos. (The color factor is obviously minimized in breeds where one coat color tends to dominate, as with Exmoors.)

> ## AT A GLANCE
>
> • The herd instinct is the strongest motivating factor in all equines.
>
> • Ponies benefit from companionship, especially that of other horses or ponies.
>
> • A successful human-pony partnership requires that you establish the leadership role.

Once every horse in the herd understands to whom he is dominant, and to whom he is subservient, daily herd life tends to be very peaceful, though skirmishes may break out when one pony decides to do some social climbing! Youngsters must carve out their position in the pecking order as they reach maturity, usually starting at the bottom. New individuals to the herd (such as might be introduced if a stallion wins a fight with a rival and acquires his harem) must also find their place. On most occasions this is accomplished with a series of meet-and-greets, threat displays, and aggressive or submissive body language rather than the tooth-and-nail fighting for which stallions are known.

The daily workings of the herd are ruled by an "alpha mare," the top-ranking female, who decides where her charges will graze, when and where they will seek water, and when they should be on the move. She is generally the strongest and most attentive member of the herd. Her function is to both guide and protect the others. The alpha mare actually has more influence on herd dynamics than the stallion, who tends to function on the fringes of the society; it is she who rules with an "iron hoof" and brooks no argument. Other herd members, however, especially those ranking just beneath her, are ever watchful for signs of weakness brought on by age or injury, and they're quick to seize power if the opportunity becomes available.

Understanding the influence of the pecking order is essen-

Herds have dominant female members.

tial if you want to establish a working relationship with a horse or pony — for he will consider you a fellow equine, whether you realize it or not. As such, he'll want to know your place in the hierarchy. As even the smallest Shetland outweighs the average human by a few hundred pounds, it's essential that we humans establish ourselves as dominant personalities in the pony/human social dynamic. We should become the "boss mares," if you will. A pony that understands and accepts that you have a higher social ranking will be a willing and cooperative companion; one who believes he ranks higher will not only be uncooperative in his training, but potentially dangerous because he has no respect for you.

When considering the herd dynamic in equine behavior, we also have to understand that one of their most pervasive motivators is fear. Like any herbivorous prey animal, a pony's senses must always be alert to potential dangers — and an alarm sent out by one pony is quickly transmitted throughout the entire herd. The equine motto is, "Panic now, think later" in times of danger, and of course, their chief defense is flight. A feral pony that ignores a rustling in the bushes may, after all, become a predator's lunch. Only when there is no other option will most ponies stand and defend themselves with hooves and teeth (and in fact, the fear of being trapped and unable to flee is also strong, which explains why so many ponies are reluctant to enter dark horse trailers and gloomy stalls).

The tendency of domestic ponies to shy, spook, and bolt at imagined dangers may be frustrating to those who are working with them, but it's a perfectly natural survival instinct, which is hard to quell. (Remember, too, that their senses of hearing and smell are far more acute than ours, and their eyesight is designed for far-sightedness, which provides them with the ability to sense perils we dumb humans can't. Often the pony that "spooks at nothing" is reacting to something very real that is outside our ability to detect.)

The ability of an alarm to travel through a herd like an electric shock holds true with human/equine relationships, as well. Ponies will very quickly pick up on the emotions of their handlers — and they will often act accordingly. A human who is sending off unconscious waves of fear or anxiety will usually find herself with a nervous pony on her hands; on the other hand, a trainer who has learned to exercise self-control and exude quiet assurance and confidence will foster these same qualities in her charges. This is just one of the reasons why losing your cool when working around ponies is never productive.

At the same time, we must realize that many of our own natural behaviors scream "predator" to a pony. Our smell, our appearance (eyes in the front of the skull, for example, a classic predator trait), and our mannerisms all tell a pony we're a threat. Given this, it's pretty remarkable (and a testament to the adaptability of ponies) that we've managed to establish a working relationship at all. We can minimize our threat displays by never moving swiftly and aggressively toward a pony, always approaching obliquely toward a pony's shoulder rather than straight at his head, and avoiding challenging eye contact. They're small gestures, but they go far toward assuring a pony that we mean no harm. (For more on equine body language and the predator/prey dynamic, you may want to study some of the principles of "natural horsemanship," promoted by many famous trainers such as John Lyons, Buck Brannaman, and Pat Parelli.)

EQUINE SOCIAL STUDIES

A pony's social life is so important to him that to be deprived of equine companionship and some sort of herd life is an extreme hardship for him.

It's true that some ponies lead satisfactory lives as solitary backyard residents, but the vast majority would be happier in a group. Not only does a pony derive a feeling of security from being in a herd, he craves physical contact with others of his kind. Watch ponies turned out together, and you'll notice they often engage in touching noses, cooperative fly-swishing (standing nose to tail with each other), and mutual grooming, nibbling each other's withers with their teeth — not to mention active play, including games of tag.

Ponies benefit from companionship.

Horses and ponies often form close friendships within the herd, pairing off with a special buddy with whom they spend most of their day. A solitary pony is generally bored, often depressed, and frequently develops destructive, neurotic habits that we call "stable vices" — things like cribbing, weaving, stall-walking, or becoming aggressive toward his handlers. So if possible, try to provide your pony with regular contact with his kin (though in a pinch, ponies will accept substitute companions, such as a goat, a donkey, a banty rooster, or a barn cat).

Ponies will also be far more content, on the whole, if they are allowed to live in a manner that mimics the way they would live in the wild. You may not have endless acreage on which they can roam, but try to provide as much turnout as possible. Living outside 24/7 isn't a hardship for most ponies; it's perfectly natural. Provided they have some shelter against the worst winter winds and rain or snow, they will thrive on such a routine.

Remember they are designed to be free-ranging, in constant motion, and almost continually grazing on low-protein, low-quality forage. Placed in a stable social dynamic (with the same turnout companions each day), they will quickly settle into a herd lifestyle, which minimizes the chance of injuries. If you find yourself feeling guilty because you think you're being cruel or neglectful of your pony if he's not in a heated barn being fed gallons of sweetfeed and getting his coat polished twice a day, remind yourself of the inherent hardiness of pony breeds and of their keen survival instincts; this is how nature designed them.

The herd lifestyle suits most equines.

The herd instinct can sometimes be used to your advantage in training a pony — employing an older, calmer pony to help establish a young one in harness, for example, or give him a lead in crossing a stream for the first time. Many activities that would cause a pony to balk become instantly more attractive if a buddy is there beside him.

THE PONY/HUMAN DYNAMIC

Establishing a dominant but trusting relationship with a pony is essential if you want to work together, but it's sometimes easier said than done. To accomplish it, you must learn to think like a pony. Your human instincts and body language will be of little value in establishing communication; he simply won't understand them. You must meet your pony on his terms, speak to him with an approximation of equine body language, and know how his thought process and his instincts work. Despite the texts that may belittle the intellect of equines when compared with dogs or cats, there's nothing stupid about a pony. He'll learn what you seek to teach him surprisingly quickly if it's presented in a format he can trust and understand, but he'll be equally quick to learn where the holes in his trainer are and take advantage of those if you let him!

Most ponies are eager to please.

Most ponies are born with a willing temperament and an eagerness to please, but there are those that will challenge human authority constantly. There are also those that, despite generations of domestication, seem inherently wary and distrustful; these can be won over only with great patience. And of course, there are also an alarming number of ponies in the world whose trust in humans has been shattered by thoughtless, ignorant, or cruel handling. Many of these can be rehabilitated by educated, kind trainers, but it's an uphill battle — and who can blame the pony for that? It's also a sad

reality of the pony world that there is a shortage of knowledgeable handlers who are of a size to work well with
ponies, especially when it comes to under-saddle training. As
a result, many ponies end up only "half-broke," confused, or
spoiled because they've been ridden only by children who
aren't experienced enough to deal with behavior problems
as they crop up. It's partly because of this syndrome that
ponies have earned a reputation for being ornery, contrary,
and willful — which in many cases is completely undeserved.

A word about gender: geldings, which have been surgically
removed from the hormonal politics of the herd, are generally considered the steadiest personalities to work with,
though it's a mistake to think that they have no place in a
herd pecking order. A lack of circulating testosterone doesn't
mean that they have no social ambitions. Some geldings are
naturally more aggressive toward others of their kind, while
others are passive and quite content to be low-ranking herd
members. Still others suffer from "delusions of stud-hood" all
of their days, apparently in denial of their altered state! But
it's absolutely preferable to geld all of the male horses in your
possession, unless you are seriously interested in getting into
the breeding game and your pony is a truly outstanding individual that will make a positive contribution to his breed.

If you do have a stallion, be aware that it may be difficult to
get him to consider you a priority when the scent of a mare
in season is in the air. Stallions tend to view all of life as an opportunity for conquest, whether territorial or sexual, and
humans can sometimes become quite forgettable in such circumstances! It's important when working with a stallion to
establish yourself very firmly as the dominant partner in the
relationship and allow no possibility that he'll ever suspect
otherwise. Some may still test you occasionally, but on the
whole if there is no threat to a stallion's sexual dominance,
he'll be quite willing to be told what to do by a "boss mare."

Mares are likely the most complex individuals with which

to work. They have a reputation for being stubborn, sulky, moody, or strong-willed — but their behavior is the normal product of strong protective maternal instincts. A mare must be constantly ready to protect her foal from danger. And like a human mother, she is a multi-tasker; she must seek food, ensure the safety of the herd, and maintain the pecking order. Given all these concerns in her daily life, it's understandable that focusing attention on her trainer isn't always going to be a top priority. She is also influenced by her heat cycle. Some mares become laid-back and placid while in season; others suffer irritability and cease to want to cooperate with anyone about anything. Mares are natural skeptics that may not immediately accept a trainer's superiority — and while their resistances may be more subtle than a stallion's, they can be far more persistent. On the other hand, many trainers have observed that once you have truly established a trusting relationship with a mare, she will give of herself far more generously than a stallion or gelding. The old saying, "You can tell a gelding, negotiate with a stallion…but you have to ask a mare" is one of the great truisms of the horse world.

Establishing yourself as the dominant partner in any human/equine relationship, regardless of the pony's gender, is largely a matter of being consistent and predictable. Your training must be based on a logical system of repetition and reward — and when you do punish, your punishment must mimic that doled out by ponies themselves in a herd situation. Watch a transgressor in the herd being disciplined and you'll see how equine justice is served: it's swiftly delivered, unequivocal, and then quickly forgotten. The human version of this may be as simple as a sharp word (a growled, "quit!" may often be enough) or a token disciplinary gesture, such as a slap to the barrel or neck with the flat of the hand. But it must be instant; a pony will not equate a delayed punishment with an action he took several minutes earlier and will just become confused and distrustful. (Most trainers do believe that correcting unwanted behavior is important, however —

simply to ignore potentially dangerous actions on the part of your pony may program him for insolence and leave you with the classic "spoiled pony.")

Rewards for jobs well done — whether a treat, a stroke on the neck, a scratch on the withers, or just a soft word of praise — must be just as instantly delivered, and far more liberally. Ponies learn largely by trial and error, and if they're given no indication that they've produced a correct response, they'll continue in confusion. Make clear what you want, acknowledge it when your pony has obliged correctly, and be willing to break each task up into smaller portions if he seems not to understand. On principles like this, trusting relationships are built.

When you run into frustrations, remember just how unnatural most of the tasks are we demand of our ponies. In the wild, the only thing likely to light on a pony's back is a cougar — the ultimate terror! Placing a saddle and a rider on a pony's back surely must go against his every survival instinct. Equally frightening is being permanently affixed to a rattling, rigid carriage, which would fatally restrict a pony's ability to escape danger in open country. We ask our ponies to leave their herds willingly to work with us, another request that is unnatural in the extrcme — and yet, they learn to subdue their fears, overrule their instincts, and happily accept the authority of man. Such trust has to be carefully fostered and never betrayed. So when your pony is uncooperative, ask yourself whether he's being obstinate or whether he's genuinely afraid or confused. The two situations are dealt with very differently — willfulness with swift (but fair) correction, fear with patience and understanding. You must establish yourself as the boss mare, it's true — but you can also be your pony's friend.

CHAPTER 8

Pony Power

What can a pony do? Virtually anything his larger cousins can! Ponies prove their versatility around the globe by participating in almost every type of equestrian work or sport. From skidding logs in the Bavarian forest to jumping cross-country fences in the American Midwest or hauling baskets of seaweed on the Japanese coast, ponies win fans for being proportionately stronger than horses, having few soundness problems, and thriving on half the feed and maintenance. For many families, a single pony can fulfill many functions — following the hounds with Dad on the weekends, pulling a Meadowbrook cart for Mom during the week, and teaching the children to ride after school — making him the ideal family companion.

Ponies can be used for many purposes, including competition.

The following are just a few of the activities in which ponies participate worldwide.

RANCH WORK

On large North American cattle ranches, Australian sheep stations, and Argentinean estancias, as well as many other farming operations around the world, a compact, muscular equine that can work all day without complaint is the rancher's biggest asset. For cowboys or gauchos, who might be dismounting and mounting several times a day to check fences or tend to livestock, a tall horse that's a struggle to get on is far from ideal...so the vast majority of true ranch horses are actually ponies, standing in the range of 14 hands or so. Some, like the Pony of the Americas, are pony breeds specifically designed for this type of work, while others are the smaller representatives of horse breeds like the American Quarter Horse, Paint, Arabian, or Appaloosa. Either way, their daily work might include fence patrol, herding or roping, cutting (separating one animal from the herd or flock), or packing supplies from one place to another. Soundness is a virtue out on the range or the outback, where veterinary assistance might be hundreds of miles away, and hardy ponies fill the bill here, too.

THE HUNTER/JUMPER RING

Many ponies are talented jumpers with a tidy style to their form over fences — knees up high, legs folded up tight as a tick, and a lovely athletic bascule (rounding of the topline from nose to tail) in the air. In the hunter ring at horse shows, ponies are divided up into small (12.2 hands or under), medium (12.3 hands to 13.2 hands), and large (13.3 hands to 14.2 hands). Courses of obstacles, usually natural materials designed to be representative of what might be encountered out foxhunting, are arranged in a pattern around the ring. The height and width of the jumps, and the distances between each of them, are adjusted to be appropriate for each size of pony. Classes are judged on the form in which the pony jumps and the steadiness of the rhythm of his canter throughout the "trip" of eight to 10 jumping efforts, as well as details like smooth turns and lead changes. Welsh ponies, whose refined good looks provide serious eye appeal, are particularly popular in the hunter ring, but many other breeds are represented as well, including cross-breds, such as Connemara/Thoroughbred crosses.

In North America, where hunter ponies may be shown only by juniors (riders under the age of 18), the show circuit culminates in the National Hunter Pony Championships and the Pony Medal Championships (in which the form of the rider is judged) at the American Horse Shows Association's Pony Finals, usually held in August. Many of the ponies that are seen at this championship show are perennial campaigners that have shown generations of kids the ropes in the show ring; it's not uncommon for good hunter ponies to continue their careers well into their 20s or 30s. Needless to say, the ones that are best at their job are worth a great deal of money.

Many ponies are talented jumpers.

The jumper ring is a variation in which style doesn't count as much as boldness and "scope" (athletic ability over fences). In a jumper class, fences are larger and more colorful, the course may be twistier and more challenging, and marks are scored purely on whether the pony jumps clear, or knocks down a rail or refuses to jump a fence, both of which incur faults. Some classes are also timed, with the fastest faultless round winning. Though the course is scaled down for the size of the pony, watching a pony jumper class is just as exciting as watching the 18-hand warmbloods of the international show-jumper ring; sometimes more so, because of the bold chances taken by impetuous young riders! Pony jumper classes are perennial favorites in the United Kingdom but have fallen out of favor in recent years in North America. The establishment of the AHSA Pony Jumper series in 1998 promises to change that; with substantial prize money offered and more classes now available nationwide, we should expect to see a resurgence in this side of the sport.

DRESSAGE

In Europe, well-schooled ponies that can perform well in the dressage ring are much valued, but in North America, the idea of training ponies specifically for this discipline is just now catching on. Dressage is often

Dressage with ponies is becoming more popular.

referred to as an art rather than a sport. Indeed, this method of training, which emphasizes the pony's natural suppleness, rhythm, relaxation, and cooperation with his rider while performing various movements on the flat (as opposed to over fences), can often look as if rider and pony are dancing. It's derived from ancient cavalry maneuvers designed to intimidate the enemy but has long since been refined into a perfectionist's form of classical riding. As such, dressage is sometimes slow to appeal to children riding ponies; they tend to crave excitement, not the perfect circle. But with wise instructors emphasizing how dressage tends to improve a pony's performance in all other aspects of his training — and with musical freestyle classes adding to the appeal — kids are catching on, and classes for juniors are increasingly popular at dressage shows. There is, of course, also nothing stopping a petite adult from showing a pony in the dressage ring, if such a mount suits her, although unfortunately some judges seem predisposed toward the enormous warmbloods that currently dominate dressage and may unfairly discount a pony.

American dressage trainer and judge Lendon Gray, who has competed at an international level aboard several pony-sized Connemaras and Connemara crosses, has recently been instrumental in establishing dressage classes specifically for ponies in the northeastern United States. She thinks judges will have a better opportunity to be objective about ponies when they are not comparing them to much larger, freer-moving warmblood breeds and hopes to eventually take the circuit nationwide.

EVENTING

Eventing is an equestrian triathlon consisting of a dressage test, a show jumping test, and an endurance test. The latter involves galloping cross-country over uneven, natural terrain and jumping immovable obstacles made from natural materials — fallen trees, stone walls, ditches, jumps built from telephone poles and railroad ties, even splashing into water jumps situated in shallow streams or ponds. Ponies and riders receive a combined score based on their performance in all three disciplines. Versatility, fitness, obedience, and boldness are required in equal portions when competing at an event or horse trials, but the scoring is based strictly on per-

Ponies of all sorts compete at eventing.

formance, not style or looks. Therefore, the sport is open to a wide variety of ponies that may not have cost big bucks or have the look of refinement needed for the hunter ring.

Many ponies and young riders get their start in eventing through the Pony Club (where an event is called a rally). An organization launched in the United Kingdom in 1929 to help children become knowledgeable and skillful horsepeople, the Pony Club now boasts chapters in more than 100 countries and a total membership of more than 100,000 riders under the age of 21. Pony Club also teaches other disciplines of English riding, and it doesn't restrict its members to riding only ponies, but it has done much to foster the sport of eventing and the natural partnership of kids and ponies over the decades.

Ponies also can compete in eventing in open competition, under the auspices of the U.S. Combined Training Association (in the United States), or through Horse Trials Canada (north of the border). There are no restrictions as to breed or size in the sport (nor are you required to be a junior to ride a pony). The vast majority of ponies compete at the lower levels, of course, where the jump sizes are appropriate for them...but a few notable ponies have climbed to the pinnacle of eventing, the Advanced level, and have competed successfully against horses nearly twice their size. Many of these have been Connemaras or Connemara crosses, which show a particular affinity for galloping and jumping cross-country. One recent example was the petite American Connemara stallion Erin Go Bragh, whose story was immortalized in a video and a collectible Breyer model for kids.

PRINCE PHILIP CUP AND OTHER MOUNTED GAMES

Combining the natural sense of fun and competitiveness among kids and ponies, mounted games foster timing, coordination, agility, sportsmanship, and an independent seat among young riders. Within the Pony Club, these games are grouped together under the banner Prince Philip Cup

Games, or PPG, and they are open to children under 15, mounted on ponies only. There are at least 41 variations on the basic races, all of which are contested by teams of five children and ponies. They include a slalom where the pair weave through a set of upright poles as quickly as possible, the perennial egg-and-spoon race (last one to retain an unbroken egg is the winner), busting balloons with a lance, carrying and dropping items into buckets, and various forms of relays. The ponies that excel at PPG tend to be quick, wiry, and on the small side (sometimes rather small for their riders, the better to facilitate quick vaulting in and out of the saddle).

The Western arena also has its version of mounted games, including timed races around three barrels arranged in a cloverleaf pattern, the "keyhole" race (in which rider and pony must sprint to the end of the arena, turn around in a very small space, and sprint back), and pole bending (weaving in and out of a line of upright poles). These are usually entered individually rather than in teams as with PPG. Because ponies rarely compete successfully against longer-strided horses, western shows often hold separate gaming classes just for ponies and restrict the age of the rider (usually under 18, as with English shows). One disadvantage is that a pony that is regularly used for gaming will tend to become very excitable, so unless his young rider is extremely competent, the pony may be quite a handful. Careful training and time away from timed events will help keep his temperament on an even keel.

PLEASURE DRIVING

Ponies have been used to pull vehicles for thousands of years, as archaeological evidence demonstrates. It is here that their small size is no disadvantage, for their proportionately greater strength allows them to pull substantial vehicles with no apparent strain. Adults who think themselves far too large to enjoy riding ponies can develop a true appreciation for them as athletes in harness. Many become enthusiastic devotees of the pony breeds as a result.

Virtually any kind of pony can excel at being driven, but certain breeds have a special reputation for being good in harness, usually because of their sprightly knee action or great weight-pulling ability. In the draft category are sturdy Haflingers, Fjords, Welsh cobs, and Dales ponies, to name a few; you may also see these breeds involved in "pony pulling contests" (a sheer test of strength) at county fairs. Other breeds, such as the Welsh, the New Forest, the Fell, and the Shetland are charming "light harness" choices — and then there are the specialists, the exaggeratedly high-stepping Hackney pony and American Shetland, which spread sparkle everywhere they go. The main requirement of any driving pony is a sensible temperament — required because in the remote location of a carriage seat, a driver has less influence over her pony than she would otherwise have mounted.

Many pleasure driving enthusiasts simply enjoy hitching up their ponies and exploring the country roads and byways, but for those with a competitive bent, there are also horse

Ponies are used for pleasure and competitive driving.

shows that specialize in driving classes and offer a place to show off a pony's obedience and charm in harness.

COMBINED DRIVING

As eventing is the adrenaline-pumped version of jumping in the hunter ring, so combined driving is the excitement-filled flip side to pleasure driving. Based on eventing and organized in a similar three-phase format with a combined score based on all three, combined driving requires driver and pony to perform a dressage test (in a large rectangular arena, at the walk and trot only), and then go cross-country over natural country (negotiating obstacles that require tight, accurate turning; tackling slopes and steps; or even splashing through water or over bridges). Finally, they compete in the "cones" phase, which tests their accuracy while driving, as efficiently as possible, between sets of traffic cones set only centimeters wider than the vehicle's wheels.

A relatively young sport, combined driving is also one of the fastest-growing equestrian disciplines in the world, with interest increasing every year. Ponies excel at combined driving, in which their toughness and agility are a major plus. Combined driving shows all feature divisions for ponies, driven singly, in pairs, and as a four-in-hand (the ultimate challenge for a reinsman!). Though the initial outlay for equipment can be considerable (especially for the cross-country phase, which requires a near-indestructible steel-framed vehicle and heavy-duty harness), combined driving remains accessible to all sorts of pony enthusiasts because your pony need not be fancy to do the job. He does, however, need to be fit and superbly well-trained — all part of the challenge of this thrilling competition.

TREKKING

If you want to experience the true roots of a pony breed, plan to go trekking in his native territory. Trekking, or long-distance trail riding, is a popular holiday activity for many people around the world. It certainly gives you a view of the countryside you'd never experience from a car — but it can also provide some wonderful insights into the ponies native to the region. If you go trekking in Scotland, you'll probably have the pleasure of being mounted on sturdy Highland ponies, which think nothing of carrying even very large adults over the rocky crags. In the lush hills of Wales, you'll more than likely be provided by your tour guide with a Welsh pony or cob, and in the Alps your equine companion may be a cheerful Haflinger. Trekking isn't limited to ponies by any means, but for many tourists, they are the ideal solution; small enough to mount easily and providing minimal intimidation to a novice rider, yet quite capable of carrying weight and hardy enough to go all day.

Ponies are also much in demand to this day as pack animals for long-distance wilderness journeys — a function not so much removed from the days when they carried coal to seaports or game home from the hills for dinner.

HARNESS RACING

Never thought of a pint-sized equine as a serious race-horse? A Trottingbred pony may change your mind. These speedy little Standardbred/Welsh or Standardbred/Shetland crosses provide racing punch in a pony-sized body, and because their upkeep is inexpensive, they bring the sport of racing to many backyard owners who could only fantasize about owning a full-sized harness horse. In places where space is limited, too, Trottingbreds win by a mile. For instance, on the tiny island of Bermuda, pony racing is thriving, with a one-fifth of a mile oval track seeing action twice a week throughout the cooler winter months. Despite their name, Trottingbreds come in both trotting and pacing varieties and often race head-to-head based on their overall speed index. Driven by both children and adults, they're becoming increasingly popular in the northeastern United States, in the eastern provinces of Canada (there are a number of breeders in Quebec), and elsewhere.

THERAPEUTIC RIDING

Almost all horsepeople know about the therapeutic effect of ponies on the human soul, but not all may realize just how much good they can do for people with physical or mental handicaps. Therapeutic riding programs, which exist all over North America and throughout the world, specialize in providing time on horseback for those with special needs — and those who work in such programs regularly witness miracles. Not only does riding stimulate muscles and nerves, and improve coordination and balance in people with deficits in these areas, it also provides an emotional connection that can bring withdrawn, frightened, even non-responsive people out of their shells and into the world.

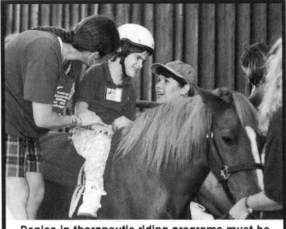

Ponies in therapeutic riding programs must be "bomb-proof."

In some ways, being a pony in a therapeutic riding program isn't terribly demanding; the vast majority of disabled riders only walk and halt with the assistance of leaders and "side-walkers" (who help the rider stay on board). In other ways, however, no job demands more of a pony. He must willingly accept the sights and sounds of braces, wheelchairs, and other paraphernalia; he must stand patiently for long periods of time, and he must be absolutely, dependably "bomb-proof." In return, of course, he'll receive as much affection as he can handle! Ponies of all shapes and sizes are useful in therapeutic programs; tiny children need a mount that's not intimidating, while larger kids and adults need a mount that can carry weight but is easy to climb up on (and not so tall that the sidewalkers have trouble fulfilling their function). Most ponies in these programs are "of a certain age" where wisdom has taken over from frivolity, and many are donated by caring owners who seek a gentle level of activity and lots of love, for their older ponies.

CHAPTER 9

The Older Pony

Most pony breeds are naturally long-lived, an indication of their inherent hardiness. And modern veterinary care, which now protects ponies from many fatal diseases with vaccinations and relieves them from the horrors of internal parasites with deworming drugs, has further enhanced their normal life spans. So it's not at all unusual for ponies to survive, and even thrive, into their 30s or 40s. For those who've formed an emotional bond with a pony, this is good news; your old friend is likely to survive to be an old, old friend and continue to bring you joy and friendship for many years.

Ponies can live to an advanced age.

But old age isn't without its difficulties. Gradually, as a pony moves past his mid-teens, age-related health problems begin to crop up. This is very individual, of course — some ponies seem as spry at 30 as they did at three, while others begin to show their age well before that. But it's fairly certain that at some point, he'll begin to suffer from some geriatric difficulties; perhaps a twinge of arthritis in his joints, which makes him stiff and creaky on cold winter mornings, or maybe a bit of a swayback (a byproduct of the gradual weakening of collagen, the body's protein scaffolding, and muscle degeneration). Cataracts may appear in his eyes, too, — they are fairly common in older horses and ponies — but while these do create a loss of transparency in the eye's lens, they rarely cause complete blindness. (Because vision is a less important sense to ponies than smell or hearing, older ponies with some impairment of vision usually cope very well.)

> ## AT A GLANCE
>
> • Many ponies live to an advanced age.
>
> • Older ponies have a number of health considerations.
>
> • Dental care is a must for older ponies because tooth deterioration can lead to eating problems.
>
> • Cushing's disease is easily recognized by a coarse, wavy coat that fails to shed in warm weather.

On the inside, more changes are afoot. Though the timing differs from pony to pony, aging inevitably results in reduced cardiopulmonary function, a decreased capacity for exercise, and impaired digestive efficiency and nutrient utilization. The immune system also takes a hit, becoming less able to defend the pony against viral and bacterial challenges — so older equines may become more prone to respiratory diseases, allergies, infected wounds, diarrhea, and surface conditions like thrush and rainrot.

Despite all this, a remarkable number of ponies remain active and useful well into their golden years, though for most, the level of intensity gradually declines. It's estimated that as the lean body mass (muscle) decreases and tendons and ligaments lose elasticity, it's speed that's the first to go, followed by agility, strength, and finally, endurance. Provided your pony is still basically sound, it's valuable to keep him working (at an appropriate level); he will maintain his condition better, keep his joints lubricated — and most ponies seem happier when they have a job to do.

Preserving your older pony's health and well-being takes increased vigilance and a little extra TLC. Here's a look at some of the most common geriatric problems you and your pony may encounter.

GETTING LONG IN THE TOOTH

First and foremost on the list is the inevitable decline of a pony's dental health. "Long in the tooth" is actually a bit of a misnomer, for while an aging pony's teeth do initially look

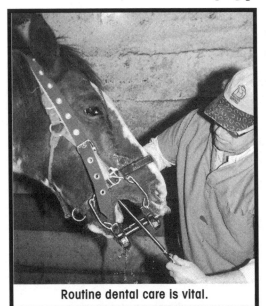
Routine dental care is vital.

"long" (in reality, it's just the angle of the incisors that changes, becoming less upright over the years and more slanted toward the horizontal), his molars, in the back of his jaw, may be wearing themselves down to tiny nubs! Throughout most of a pony's life, the teeth continually erupt from the gum surface, much like a rodent's (and quite unlike our own), but somewhere in his mid-20s he may run out of choppers. From then on, he'll continue to wear the existing surfaces down until, if he lives long enough, he may end up with nothing with which to chew. As more of the roots become exposed, the teeth also can be prone to being lost. In addition, his sloping incisors (vital to tearing off grass and forage from the ground) become far less efficient at biting down and tearing fibrous foodstuffs.

"Hooks" on the molars, a problem for all domestic ponies throughout their lives, can compound the dental problems of an older pony (and are especially likely if he has not had the benefit of routine — and thorough — "floating" as he has aged). Older ponies also can suffer from broken teeth, usually the result of trauma. Long-term mouth infections occur, too, and may result in gum abscesses or lost teeth.

The loss of a molar or pre-molar may reduce the ability of the pony to chew his feed. When a gap develops, the opposing teeth tend to grow into the space, interrupting the normal grinding surfaces of the upper and lower arcades of molars. If an incisor or incisors are lost, your pony may not be able to graze efficiently — so don't depend on pasture to help him maintain condition.

All of these dental problems may lead to a loss of appetite (who wants to eat when your mouth hurts?) or poorly chewed food that may fall out of your pony's mouth in "quids." That food that does get swallowed is often poorly digested because it is in larger-than-normal chunks that the digestive system may not be able to break down.

You can't prevent the normal wear-and-tear on your pony's teeth (even if you could, that would cause another whole set of problems). And equine dentures are still a fantasy for the future. But there is much your veterinarian can do to help keep your pony's mouth in its best possible condition as he ages. Scheduling a complete dental checkup at least once every six months is crucial. Your pony may not require "floating" (filing down the sharp edges and hooks with a metal rasp) each time you check, but the examination will allow your veterinarian to monitor changes and treat any problems promptly, before they seriously compromise your pony's health.

Ask your veterinarian to pay special attention to the molars at the very back of the jaw, where hooks and points often get neglected. The use of a speculum (a fearsome-looking, but harmless instrument that helps hold the pony's jaws open while your veterinarian examines him) is essential for a thorough job, so ask specifically for it. And monitor your pony's condition closely; if he begins to show a lack of enthusiasm for his feed, a loss of weight, "quidding," or if he suddenly objects to being bridled or even brushed around his face, suspect dental problems and consult your vet promptly.

DIGESTIVE INEFFICIENCY

An older pony's metabolism is somewhat slower than a young pony's, and his more modest energy expenditure should mean that his baseline requirement for calories is lower than it was in his early years. Unfortunately, there are other factors at work that cancel out this effect. Studies have demonstrated that the geriatric pony often suffers from decreased digestive efficiency: his gastrointestinal tract becomes less able to process and extract the nutrients from his feed, so many essential dietary ingredients fail to be absorbed and instead pass through the body untouched. Older ponies probably experience a decrease in stomach acid and enzymes, too, and decreased motility in their intestinal tracts.

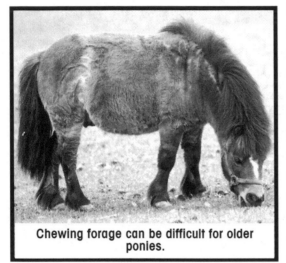

Chewing forage can be difficult for older ponies.

The combined effect of this is that geriatric ponies have trouble absorbing some, but not all, nutrients. Research has indicated that the absorption of protein (essential for the repair of bones and soft tissues) and phosphorus (involved in the strength and resilience of bone, as well as a number of maintenance functions at the cellular level) are compromised in older equines, and that, as a result, the requirement for both these nutrients is increased as a pony gets older. Calcium absorption does not appear to be affected, but if you increase the amount of phosphorus in the diet, it's a good idea to increase the amount of calcium as well, in order to maintain that all-important calcium:phosphorus ratio of 1:1 or better.

The ability to digest carbohydrates (grains) doesn't seem to be compromised in older ponies, but the ability to digest fiber *is* — and since fiber is the foundation of any pony's diet, that's a significant problem. Researchers suspect that the difficulty is two-fold: first, many older ponies find it hard to chew forage properly, especially when it is fibrous, long-stem hay instead of sweet, young grass; and second, a less varied and less efficient population of microorganisms in the colon may make for a less thorough job of fiber fermentation and nutrient extraction.

The ability to manufacture or absorb certain vitamins also seems to decrease as ponies age. It's suspected that the decrease of gut microflora compromises the ability of the pony to manufacture his own B vitamins (normally produced in abundance), as well as vitamin C (ascorbic acid), which is important for the pony's immune function.

CHOKE

Very old ponies that have become essentially toothless run an increased risk of choke, an alarming condition in which less-than-thoroughly-chewed food becomes lodged in the esophagus. Equine anatomy differs from ours, so when a pony suffers from choke he's in no danger of suffocating, but he will still be in considerable distress as he tries to dislodge the blockage. Food particles and saliva may dribble from his nostrils, and he may panic and thrash. If you suspect your pony is choking, call your veterinarian immediately; he or she may decide to pass a naso-gastric tube down your pony's throat and pour down small amounts of water or mineral oil in an effort to soften the blockage and get it moving again.

Prevention is definitely the best course when it comes to choke. If your pony has trouble chewing his food or has previously suffered an episode of choke, you need to alter his feeding routine. Instead of offering long-stem hay, try hay cubes or pellets soaked in water to make an easy-to-chew mush. Soaked sugar beet pulp is also a good fiber source that is soft and easy to chew. If you are feeding grain, consider switching from whole grains or sweetfeed to a pelleted or extruded feed that has been soaked in water for an hour or so before feeding. Even very ancient ponies can often be maintained quite well on such regimens for many years.

ARTHRITIS

Arthritis, an inflammation or degeneration of the tissues associated with the joints, eventually catches up with almost every pony. A chronic degenerative condition of the cartilage associated with the ends of bones, arthritis compromises the ability of the joints to flex or to bear weight and can sometimes be crippling. For some older ponies, the symptoms remain mild: perhaps a little stiffness after a night of inactivity in a stall, which he'll warm out of as he begins to move. For others, arthritis may express itself in lameness-causing conditions such as ringbone and bone spavin.

If caught in its early stages, arthritis often can be successfully managed with injectible therapies such as polysulfated glucosaminoglycans (PSGAGs — brand name Adequan) or sodium hyaluronate. These drugs were originally designed to be administered intra-articularly (into the joint), but this method is risky because there's the chance of introducing infectious organisms into the joint space. Fortunately, both have now been demonstrated to have the same effects when admin-

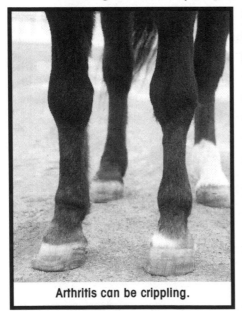
Arthritis can be crippling.

istered intravenously or intra-muscularly. There are also a wide range of oral supplements available with similar ingredients (usually glucosamine and/or chondroitin sulfate), but the evidence supporting their effectiveness is sparse. It's fairly clear that they do no harm, but they are far from inexpensive; the injectible formulations have far more research behind them for the price.

Providing a maximum amount of turn-out is important for arthritic ponies, as moving about helps them lubricate their joints. Anti-inflammatory drugs, certain changes in farriery, and extra-deep bedding (and soft footing if he continues to work) can also do much to make an old and arthritic pony more comfortable. And it's crucial that you not let him become obese, as the extra weight only increases the stress on the legs.

In addition to arthritis in the joints, the tendons and ligaments of older ponies often lose elasticity, while cartilage replacement in the joints slows — all conditions that can interfere with an older pony's mobility, enthusiasm for exercise, and stability.

KIDNEY AND LIVER DISEASE

Decreased kidney and/or liver function are rare, but not unheard of, problems in geriatric ponies.

When the kidneys don't function as they should, the first signs are usually weight loss and a loss of appetite. Though these symptoms may sound rather mild, they should not be taken lightly, because kidney failure can be fatal. Here's why: Horses and ponies are unique among animals in that they get rid of excess dietary calcium in the urine rather than in the manure. When the kidneys aren't working correctly, calcium (in the form of calcium oxalate) builds up in the kidney tissue, the urethra, or the bladder, rather than being excreted. These stones can be extremely painful, and of course they often interfere with normal urinary function, which makes it impossible for the pony's body to rid itself of toxins. (Those in the bladder or urethra can sometimes be surgically removed, but those in the kidney are inoperable.) There is also the potential for calcium to build up to potentially lethal levels in the bloodstream.

Ponies with kidney disease need to be placed on a low calcium diet (less than 0.45% of the overall ration), and protein and phosphorus should also be reduced (to less than 10%, and less than 0.3%, respectively), contrary to the usual recommendations for older ponies. Avoid feeding legume hays, such as alfalfa or clover, and beet pulp (both have too high a calcium content), as well as wheat bran (its phosphorus level is too high). Focus instead on grass hay and, if you feed grain, choose cracked corn, or a complete pelleted ration with under 10% protein.

Ponies with liver disease may suffer from jaundice (a yellowing of the mucous membranes and the whites of the eyes), weight loss, lethargy, loss of appetite, and an intolerance for fat and protein in the diet. Severely affected ponies also may be irritable and circle aimlessly or press their heads against objects. In contrast to kidney failure, ponies with liver problems need increased sugar in their diets in order to maintain blood glucose levels. Their diets should emphasize carbohydrates and de-emphasize protein and fats. Base the diet on processed (not whole) corn or milo (also known as sorghum), or a low-protein sweetfeed or pellet, as well as low-protein grass hay and/or beet pulp.

Because the liver is also a site of the synthesis of B vitamins (especially niacin) and vitamin C, ponies with liver dysfunction should be fed a diet supplemented with oral B-complex (about 5 cc a day) and ascorbic acid.

Your veterinarian can diagnose kidney or liver dysfunction with the help of a blood test.

TUMORS

It's estimated that some sort of tumor is present in 70% of horses and ponies over the age of 20. Fortunately, in most cases these growths are benign rather than malignant. Tumors on the pituitary and thyroid glands are probably the most common tumors in geriatrics (more on these in a moment).

Other types include abdominal fat lipomas, which are not malignant but can cause problems because they tend to grow on slender stalks that can wrap around portions of the intestine and obstruct the flow of blood and abdominal contents. If detected, these growths can sometimes be removed laparoscopically, potentially saving your pony from a severe case of colic.

Skin melanomas are also common problems, particularly in gray (and occasionally pinto) ponies. We're still not sure why, but nearly 80% of gray ponies over the age of 15 years are affected by melanomas, those dark lumps that usually sprout under the tail and in the peri-anal region. They are generally benign, but they do become malignant and invasive on occasion. If a melanoma spreads to the abdominal region, a pony usually will begin to lose weight and condition, become debilitated, and suffer from fluid collection in the abdomen. Large growths may impinge on the blood supply, the nerves, or the intestinal tract. In some cases they can be removed, but they often recur.

THYROID TUMORS

One of the most common tumors in geriatric ponies is a benign growth on the thyroid, a small gland roughly in the area of the throatlatch. The growth sometimes can be palpated as a firm, smooth mass just under the skin, somewhere along the upper third of the trachea (windpipe).

A pony with a thyroid tumor is at increased risk of obesity and founder, and may suffer from hypothyroidism (a condition in which the thyroid no longer secretes enough of its hormones, resulting in lethargy, a potbellied appearance, muscular weakness, and a poor immune response). Fortunately, many of these ponies respond well to daily doses of powdered synthetic thyroid hormone.

Studies have suggested that older geldings and stallions seem to be at higher risk for thyroid tumors than mares.

CUSHING'S SYNDROME

Ponies with Cushing's syndrome (named for turn-of-the-century American surgeon Harvey Cushing, who researched

Older ponies often suffer from Cushing's syndrome.

the human brain and pituitary gland) are easily recognized by a heavy, coarse, wavy coat that fails to shed in the summer (occurring in more than 85% of cases). They also suffer from polydipsia (excessive thirst) coupled with polyuria (excessive urination), a swaybacked or potbellied appearance, increased appetite (generally with no corresponding weight gain), and chronic laminitis.

Because their immune systems are compromised, ponies with Cushing's syndrome become more susceptible to bouts of respiratory disease, skin infections, foot abscesses, buccal (mouth) ulcers, periodontal disease, large loads of internal parasites, and even infections of the tendon sheath or joints. Wound healing is also noticeably slowed.

Some ponies with Cushing's become lethargic or depressed. Less commonly, a mare's estrous cycle can be suppressed or abnormal, and she may even produce milk without being pregnant.

At the heart of equine Cushing's is a pituitary adenoma, a benign tumor on this marble-sized gland at the base of the brain. The pituitary is responsible for the regulation of almost all of the body's hormonal systems, so when its function is compromised, there's a ripple effect throughout the pony's whole body. In simple terms, the pituitary gland no longer properly regulates the secretion of cortisol from the adrenal glands, perched on top of the kidneys. As a result, levels of cortisol in the pony's system can rise dramatically, and this causes the symptoms of Cushing's.

Over the course of months or years, the tumor may grow to the point where it puts pressure on the adjacent hypothalamus, which controls thermoregulation (among other things); some researchers think this may be the reason behind the growth of the characteristic heavy hair coat. The tumor also could eventually press on the optic nerve, which lies close by the pituitary, causing blindness. Other symptoms of very advanced Cushing's include head-tilting and dementia.

In humans, Cushing's syndrome is sometimes correctable by surgery or radiation treatments. But in ponies, surgery, unfortunately, is not an option. Not only is the pituitary gland just about as inaccessible as it could get, but a pony with a pituitary adenoma usually is over 20, already has a compromised immune system, and is a very poor bet for surviving a general anesthetic. Therefore, drug therapies are the treatment of choice for equine Cushing's.

There are two drugs that have been used to reverse some or all of the symptoms of Cushing's. One is cyproheptadine, a seratonin blocker that helps normalize cortisol levels in the blood and is available in an easily absorbed, tablet form. The dosage of this drug has to be regulated carefully by your veterinarian to first make an impact on the symptoms, then reduced to a maintenance level. During the first few weeks Cushingoid ponies receive cyproheptadine, owners commonly report that symptoms, such as the heavy hair coat and potbelly, disappear, and their ponies regain their vigor and muscle tone.

Newer to the field of Cushing's treatment is pergolide mesylate (trade name Permax), a dopamine agonist that is also

Treating Cushing's requires careful management.

used to treat human Parkinson's disease. At low dosages (compared to those administered to humans), Permax often triggers positive responses within three weeks or so. Like cyproheptadine, it can be administered orally as a tasteless tablet that can be crushed and mixed with a little molasses.

When deciding whether to medicate a Cushing's pony, you must take into account the condition of the pony. Ponies whose symptoms are fairly mild definitely respond best to the medication and might have their useful lives extended by a number of years; but a pony that is already suffering from chronic founder and recurrent infections might derive limited benefit. Neither drug is inexpensive, and the pony will likely need to remain on the medication for the remainder of his life.

It is also worth remembering that none of these drug therapies addresses the root of the problem, the pituitary tumor itself. They merely treat the symptoms, and the tumor itself will continue to grow until at last it compromises the pony's quality of life enough that euthanasia is the kindest answer. Methods of removing or stopping the growth of pituitary adenomas are still, unfortunately, in the future of veterinary medicine.

Maintaining a pony with Cushing's syndrome will require you to focus on careful health management and preventative care. Particular attention should be paid to helping out the immune system with vaccinations, deworming, dental care, and prompt response to any developing infections. Some Cushingoid ponies may require body-clipping in the summer months, and they should be provided with shelter and/or blankets in winter. Those with laminitis will require ongoing and expert farrier care, as well. All of these considerations, however, may be worth it to owners who feel strongly about maintaining the health of a treasured old friend.

LOSS OF CONDITION

Obviously there are a number of factors that can contribute to a pony's weight loss. Some, which we've already discussed, are physical, but you may want to consider the psychological as well.

For example, consider that older ponies are, as a rule, less aggressive than younger ones — so if they are fed in a group situation, they might be pushed aside and be unable to eat all they should. Second, they tend to suffer more than younger ponies from stress factors. Hard work, being shipped for long distances, or just being chased around the field by his more exuberant pasture buddies — all can take a toll on the aging pony and cause him to lose his appetite (a condition clinically called anorexia). In general, it takes less to make an older pony lose his enthusiasm for his meals; even water that is too cold (causing tooth pain) might be enough.

Extremes of weather can be particularly hard for geriatric ponies. As they age, they have trouble with thermoregulation (the body's ability to maintain its internal temperature). As a result, your older pony may require more food energy in bitter winter conditions; in some instances, you may have to increase the calorie content of his feed to help him maintain his condition in winter. Though ordinarily ponies have little need of blankets, your geriatric friend may be grateful for some artificial protection on the most blustery or wet winter days. Providing a good windbreak or shelter in his pasture will also help. In hot, humid conditions, ponies also can lose their appetites; so if necessary, body-clip your octogenarian and consider giving him a cooling mist with the hose when he is looking particularly uncomfortable. Some farms in southern climates even rig up irrigation hoses on fence lines that can spray cool water on the herd several times a day.

Many stress factors can be reduced with some basic management changes, such as putting your older pony in a pasture with others of a similar age rather than rambunctious youngsters. When you feed him, isolate him in a separate paddock or stall so that he doesn't have to compete for his meals. Making every effort to keep his appetite good is crucial, because once an older pony gets skinny, it can be a real struggle to put weight back on him.

Be willing to experiment to find out what your older pony likes and what he finds easy to eat. And, of course, make sure he always has access to unlimited amounts of fresh water, as no pony maintains a good appetite when he's dehydrated. In the winter, serving warm water has been shown to increase water intake dramatically; just like you, your pony may be reluctant to drink ice-cold water on a frigid day! Cater to his dwindling interest in food by offering small meals more often, and tempt him with soft flavor enhancers like molasses or applesauce if necessary.

SUCH SWEET SORROW

Though the focus of this chapter has been the successful management of the aging process, there comes a time for every pony when the accumulated wear and tear becomes too much. A dwindling appetite, chronic pain, immobility (or a lack of desire to move), and self-imposed isolation from the herd and from humans — any or all of these symptoms can tell you that your pony's systems are shutting down. When that fateful day arrives, humane euthanasia is the most generous final gift you can give your old friend.

But just so we don't finish on that sad note — remember that ponies who have been gently started, well cared-for throughout their lives, and exercised consistently (but not overworked) can enjoy longer and healthier lives than ever before. As the years go by, you may have to adapt your demands to your pony's capabilities, but any diminished performance ambitions will likely be more than compensated for by the enjoyment you get out of your relationship with an older pony. They are truly worth their weight in gold.

INDEX

RECOMMENDED READINGS

Briggs, K. *Understanding Equine Nutrition*. Lexington, Ky:The Blood-Horse, Inc., 1998.

Grove, K. *Field Guide to Horses*. Edmonton, Alberta: Lone Pine Publishing, 1998.

Holland, RE. *Understanding the Older Horse*. Lexington, Ky: The Blood-Horse, Inc., 1999.

Lewis, LD. *Feeding and Care of the Horse*, 2nd ed. Baltimore: Williams and Wilkins, 1996.

McBane, S. *Know Your Pony*. London: Ward Lock, 1992, 1995.

McCarthy, GB. *Practical Horse and Pony Nutrition*. London: J.A. Allen, 1998.

McDonnell, S. *Understanding Horse Behavior*. Lexington, Ky: The Blood-Horse, Inc., 1999.

Pittenger, PJ. *The Wonderful World of Ponies*. New York: Arco Publishing, 1969, 1973.

Redden, R. *Understanding Laminitis*. Lexington, Ky: The Blood-Horse, Inc., 1998.

Wiederhold, H. *Your Pony Book*, revised edition. New York: Bonanza Books, 1966.

Pony sites on the Internet

Comprehensive alphabetical listing of horse and pony breeds, from Oklahoma State University, with links to many breed association web sites: http://www.ansi.okstate.edu/breeds/horses

Breeds of the world, by continent or alphabetically, from the International Museum of the Horse: http://imh.org/exhibits/past/breeds-of-the-world

United States Pony Club: http://www.ponyclub.org

The Pony Club (Great Britain): http://www.pony-club.org.uk

Canadian Pony Club: http://www.canadianponyclub.org

United States Combined Training Association: http://www.eventingusa.com

United States Dressage Federation: http://www.usdf.org

The Mounted Games Association: http://mounted-games.org

The National 4-H web site: http://www.4-h.org

The Canadian 4-H Council: http://www.4-h-canada.ca

The Horse Interactive: http://www.thehorse.com

Picture Credits

CHAPTER 1
Tom Hall, 8; CLiX Photography, 10.

CHAPTER 2
Stephanie Church, 13.

CHAPTER 3
Anne M. Eberhardt, 31, 34, 35, 37; Nanette T. Rawlins, 38.

CHAPTER 4
CLiX Photography, 40, 43, 44.

CHAPTER 5
Ric Redden, DVM, 50; Kendra Bond, 52.

CHAPTER 6
Anne M. Eberhardt, 59, 64, 65; Barbara D. Livingston, 60; Marlyn Exmoors, 65;
CLiX Photography, 66, 67, 68, 70; Dusty L. Perin, 68; Nanette T. Rawlins, 69;
Gemma Giannini, 71; Pony of the Americas Club, 72; Barbara D. Livingston, 72.

CHAPTER 7
CLiX Photography, 76, 78; Nancy Stevens-Brown, 78; Gemma Giannini, 79.

CHAPTER 8
Tim Brockhoff, 84; CLiX Photography, 86-88, 91; Siegel Photography, 94.

CHAPTER 9
E. Matthew Goins, 96; Toddypix, 98, 106; Barbara D. Livingston, 100;
CLiX Photography, 102.

EDITOR — JACQUELINE DUKE
ASSISTANT EDITOR — JUDY L. MARCHMAN
COVER/BOOK DESIGN — SUZANNE C. DEPP
COVER PHOTO — GEMMA GIANNINI

About the Author

Karen Briggs, B.Sc., is a career horsewoman, who began riding at the age of eight and didn't, as her parents had hoped, "grow out of it." As an equine nutritionist and horse feed specialist for United Cooperatives of Ontario, a large feed company, she was responsible for researching, designing, and marketing a new line of premium quality feeds for performance, pleasure, and breeding horses, and for provid-

Karen Briggs

ing common-sense nutritional information and ration balancing to customers across the province of Ontario. She is also a Canadian Equestrian Federation certified riding instructor, and has managed farms and riding schools in both Canada and Bermuda.

Over the past 20 years, Karen has worked at both Standardbred and Thoroughbred racing stables, and competed in disciplines as diverse as Western pleasure, competitive trail, and dressage. She currently concentrates on three-day eventing, and provides nutritional advice on a consulting basis, as well as writing for more than 20 American, Canadian, and European equine magazines. She is the author of *Understanding Equine Nutrition,* part of the Horse Health Care Library, and a frequent contributor to *The Horse: Your Guide To Equine Health Care*.